# GALATIANS, EPHESIANS, PHILIPPIANS & COLOSSIANS:

## A Daily Dialogue with God

### 54 studies & readings

written & edited by
**Whitney Kuniholm**

*with Reflections from Scripture Union*

Harold Shaw Publishers
Wheaton, Illinois

*For Roland and Althea*

*"Reflections" are based upon notes by the following
authors: for Galatians, P. E. Knight, A. Morgan Derham,
Raymond Brown; for Ephesians, John Young, Tony
Capon; for Philippians, A. Morgan Derham, Raymond
Brown, Gordon Harman; for Colossians, Tony Capon,
A. Morgan Derham, Myron Augsburger; used by per-
mission of Scripture Union, 1716 Spruce St., Philadel-
phia, Penna. 19103.*

*ISBN 0-87788-292-4*

*Printed in the United States of America*

*89  88  87  86  85  84  83  7  6  5  4  3  2  1*

# Contents

# How to Use This Book

What you are about to do in the following pages is not just study the Bible. That's only part of it. You see, God speaks directly to you through the words of the Bible. And in prayer, you can speak to him. As you learn to perform these two activities together you'll discover a dynamic, two-way communication with God.

Each two-page daily study is built around a simple yet profound four-step formula: *Pray, Read, Meditate, Pray.*

## ☐ PRAY

Ask the Holy Spirit to help you understand and apply what you are about to read. You may pray the written prayer or simply use it as a guide to your own prayer. Ask for a sharp mind and an open, honest heart. Remember, God *wants* to speak to you through his Word.

## ☐ READ

When you read the passage for the day, read it slowly and deeply. Resist the temptation to think, "Oh, I know what these verses say because I've read them so many times." Try reading the passage several times to make sure you get it all. Don't expect to hear God's still small voice if you whisk through the verses in a few seconds.

## ☐ MEDITATE

Don't be scared off by the word meditate. It definitely does not mean Eastern meditation where the goal is simply to empty yourself. Rather, Christian meditation consists of pushing away your day-to-day thoughts and worries in order to fill yourself with thoughts of God and his Word. This studyguide will help you meditate on God's Word with the following features:

*Discovery.* Use your God-given intellect and carefully answer the four questions for each day, referring to the excerpts from commentaries when you need to. But don't parrot the answers you've heard others give or that you think are correct or that sound good. Find your own answers. What does the text actually say? What does it mean? What does it mean to you? How does it apply to your life?

*Reflection.* After working through the passage on your own, read the comments on the verses. See if your personal discoveries are confirmed or if your hanging questions are answered. Also, see if the Reflection touches on something you've overlooked or gives you a new insight.

*My Response.* Next, you come to an important feature: your response to what you have learned. Here you have an opportunity to express whatever is on your heart and mind. You may want to write out your praise and thanks to God based on what you have read or you may want to respond to God's Word by writing down a specific way you plan to apply what you've learned. Or you may simply want to crystalize what you feel is the most memorable truth of the day's passage. But after listening to God speak to you through reading the Scriptures, answering questions and reading the Reflection, you need to begin *your* part of the "conversation."

*Memory Point.* To reinforce the theme of each chapter, a Key Verse has been selected. The Memory Point for each day gives you a short suggestion to help you memorize or review the verse. God's Word, committed to instant recall, can straighten your mental perspective, meet your emotional needs, and repel the Enemy's attacks. The ten Key Verses are printed on the last two pages of this book. Each is printed from the NIV, and there is also a space for you to write in another translation of each verse, if you prefer. You'll want to refer back to this page often since memorization requires regular review.

## ☐ PRAY
Finally, pray again for help in applying God's Word. If you truly believe the Bible is God's Word and that God does speak to you in it, then you must respond. And that's not always easy, but God will give you the ability and even the desire to do what he wants if you ask him. The prayer suggestions will help you get started, but don't stop there! Your prayer can and should also proceed to confession, thanksgiving or praise, and intercession.

## ☐ Bonus Features
At the back of the book you will find two additional features that will enhance your walk with God and help you keep a record of what he is doing in your life.

*Prayer Notebook.* Some Christians think, "I know God answers prayer, but I don't often see it." The problem most of us have is that God answers many of our prayers, but we simply forget! By keeping track of your prayer life you will see how God *is* answering your prayers. When you have a request you want to bring to the Lord, jot it down in your Prayer Notebook along with the date. Then begin praying about it. When God answers, according to his own time schedule, record the date you receive the answer.

*God Is Speaking To Me About . . .* This is your opportunity to record major spiritual breakthroughs as well as key actions you are prompted to take whose date you want to recall. For example, you may sense God's direction to reach out to a certain neighbor, or you may receive a new insight into the meaning of your relationship with God. Record these insights in this special section you'll find at the back of this book.

As he studied the book of Galatians, the eyes of Martin Luther were opened to the significance of the Christian's justification by faith. Your insights may not change the entire church, but they will alter your life and probably those around you.

## ☐ Tips for Daily Bible Study

Daily Bible study and prayer are essential if you are to grow to be a stronger, more joyful Christian. Here are six tips that will help you:

**1. *Make a Commitment.*** Put your decision to have daily Bible study and prayer in writing, on a 3x5 card or at the front of this book. Tell your spouse or close friend of your commitment and ask him or her to check up on you occasionally. Finally, tell God of your commitment and ask for his help in sticking to it.

**2. *Use a Bible that is clear to you.*** Since so many good translations are available today, find one that you enjoy and trust. Occasionally try a new version for familiar passages. Of course you cannot use this book without your Bible.

All quotes are from the *New International Version* unless otherwise noted. However, special care has been taken to make this studyguide usable with any Bible version, traditional or contemporary.

**3. *Establish a routine.*** Plan to study God's Word at the same time each day. Find a spot where you can be alone. Keep your Bible, this book, and a pen together in one place so you don't have to hunt for them. Daily Bible study becomes easier when it's part of your daily schedule.

**4. *Don't let guilt impede your progress.*** There will be days when you can't keep up your normal schedule. Don't listen to Satan's accusations at times like that; simply pick up where you left off.

**5. *Expect to meet God.*** The purpose for daily Bible study is not to become a Bible know-it-all or to prove that you are a super-Christian or to fulfill some obligation. Knowing God better and growing in your relationship should be your goal.

**6. *Plan to keep going.*** Don't let the end of this book be the end of a daily time for reading, meditation, and prayer. Get another studyguide or set up your own study schedule. As you soak in God's Word daily your life becomes fertile soil which God can use to create beautiful new growth.

## ☐ Have a Good Time

Finally, have fun! Too many Christians think of daily Bible study as drudgery. That's just the lie that Satan wants you to believe. You may have to work at sticking to your commitment, but if you stick with it, you'll find your daily appointment with God is the most rewarding part of your Christian life. Nothing is more exciting than hearing God speak directly to you through his Word, and enjoying the privilege of two-way communication with your Creator and Lord.

# Introduction to Galatians, Ephesians, Philippians & Colossians

## ☐ The Author

The apostle Paul was the workhorse of the first-century church. He traveled, preached, and wrote with unfailing energy and enthusiasm. He earned his own support when possible, was beaten and rejected, thrown in jail and taken to court. When he was released he went right back to what had gotten him into trouble—proclaiming the gospel. Later he was rearrested and probably died around 67 A.D. at the hands of the Roman emperor Nero.

Despite struggles and losses he was able to establish many churches all over the Mediterranean world. And to make sure these groups remained faithful to Jesus Christ, Paul wrote a number of letters, four of which you are about to study.

## ☐ Overview of Galatians: Defending the Gospel

Galatia was a Roman province in the area that lies between the Mediterranean and Black Sea. On his first missionary journey Paul visited several of the towns in the southern region of Galatia (Antioch, Iconium, Lystra and Derbe). Later Paul wrote to the churches he had just visited because he had heard they were in danger of giving in to pressure that would alter the gospel he had planted. This pressure came about because of Jew/Gentile tensions. Jews and Gentiles had always remained separate and contemptuous of each other. But in Christ they were suddenly united and equal recipients of God's blessing. However, some Jewish Christians were trying to impose the old Mosaic Law (specifically circumcision) on the Gentile believers as a prerequisite for salvation. So when Paul returned to Antioch after completing his first missionary journey around 49 A.D. and heard about these Judaizing pressures, he dashed off a passionate letter to defend the gospel message he had preached in Galatia.

Paul's defense was threefold: personal, theological, and moral. Because the Judaizers were trying to discredit Paul behind his back, he opened the letter by firmly establishing his apostolic authority (chapters 1 and 2). He then turned his attention to the theological implications of the Judaizers' teachings and in so doing established the principle of justification by faith (chapters 3 and 4). Finally, Paul spelled out the moral implications of faith in Jesus by giving a richly detailed explanation of true freedom in Christ (chapters 5 and 6).

In Galatians we sense the power of the apostle Paul's personality. He was sometimes angry, at other times exasperated; sometimes humble, yet often incredibly bold. But all the time he was committed to one goal: convincing his readers that the way to God is not through some combination of Christianity and Judaism or Christianity *plus* anything else, but rather through faith in Christ alone.

## *Outline of Galatians*
I. Personal Defense
   A. Greeting and purpose for writing  *1:1–10*
   B. Paul's gospel explained  *1:11–24*
   C. Paul's gospel tested  *2:1–21*
II. Theological Defense
   A. Abraham and God  *3:1–14*
   B. Law and faith  *3:15–4:31*
III. Moral Defense
   A. Freedom in Christ  *5:1–26*
      1. Don't lose it  *1–12*
      2. Don't abuse it  *13–26*
   B. Final instructions  *6:1–18*

## ☐ Overview of Ephesians: God's Plan in Christ
Ephesus was the leading city in the Roman province of Asia. It was a natural meeting point for ships from Rome and caravans from Asia and therefore became a prosperous commercial port. Ephesus was also a center for pagan worship, the main attraction being the temple containing a statue of the goddess Diana who, its worshipers claimed, had fallen from the sky.

Paul briefly visited Ephesus on his second missionary journey (52 A.D.) and left there Aquila and Priscilla, the ones who probably brought the gospel to that city. On his third missionary journey, however, Paul stayed in Ephesus much longer, over two years. In Acts 19, Luke reported some of the events that occurred during this time, including a massive riot caused by the fact that Christians had put a damper on the lucrative silver idol business. After that, Paul departed from Ephesus, leaving Timothy there to lead the church.

Paul wrote his letter to the Ephesians several years after his visits, in 62 A.D., from a prison in Rome as he neared the end of his life. An interesting detail about the letter is that in the oldest copies of it there is a blank space instead of the words "in Ephesus" in verse 1. This may have meant that Paul intended it to be a "circular letter," providing space for a messenger to fill in the name of any city to which he was traveling. This explanation would account for its formal, less personal tone.

The message of the letter centers on God's great plan of salvation. Paul's repeated use of the phrase "in Christ" or "in him" is the key that explains God's plan of salvation. To summarize, Paul says that *in Christ* we receive great spiritual blessings, a basis for unity, and a new standard for living. Generally, the first half of

Ephesians is theological, while the second half is practical (a reminder that a healthy Christian life requires a balance between the two).

### Outline of Ephesians
I. Blessings in Christ
   A. A list of blessings  *1:1-14*
   B. A prayer for growth  *1:15-23*
   C. The facts of new life  *2:1-10*
II. Unity in Christ
   A. Jews and Gentiles  *2:11-22*
   B. Paul's task and prayer  *3:1-21*
   C. The church's unity and diversity  *4:1-16*
III. Living in Christ
   A. Imitators of God  *4:17-5:20*
   B. Christian households  *5:21-6:9*
   C. The Christian's defense  *6:10-24*

### □ Overview of Philippians: Paths to Joy
During Paul's second missionary journey he had a vision of a man begging him to "come over to Macedonia and help us" (Acts 16:6-10). As a result, Paul soon found himself in Philippi, the major city of the region, aggressively preaching and teaching the gospel.

His efforts, as usual, met with stiff resistance. Paul and his companion Silas were beaten and thrown into prison. However, God worked in this situation to further spread the gospel using an earthquake and an unexpected opportunity to witness to the Roman guards (Acts 16:16-40). After demanding his rights as a Roman citizen, Paul was released from prison. He then left Philippi, leaving Luke to lead the young church. Paul returned to Philippi several times and developed a close bond with the Christians there.

His letter to the Philippians was written later, from prison (Phil. 1:12-26; 2:17). The question scholars have asked is, "which prison?" Some suggest Paul wrote Philippians while in prison at Caesarea; others say Rome; still others say it was during his captivity in Ephesus. Each theory has its own list of evidences, though the question and its answer are not of crucial importance. The most popular view, however, is that Paul wrote Philippians while imprisoned in Rome.

The purpose of the letter was to thank the Philippian Christians for a financial gift they had sent, which Paul did at the end of the letter. He used the occasion to explain some deeper truths about the Christian life. Although his style was somewhat rambling and not systematically organized, he did emphasize the need to imitate Christ and work at making him Lord of all.

Philippians is a personal letter and Paul's concern and love for his readers is apparent. The quality of joy also reverberates throughout the letter. Even while locked in prison, Paul was able to maintain and even spread the joy of knowing Christ. His example stands as one of the most powerful messages of the book.

**Outline of Philippians**
I. Imitating Christ
   A. Thanksgiving and prayer  *1:1–11*
   B. Paul's example  *1:12–30*
   C. The humility of Christ  *2:1–18*
   D. Timothy and Epaphroditus  *2:19–30*
II. Living for the Lord
   A. New priorities  *3:1–11*
   B. Pressing on  *3:12–21*
   C. Rejoicing  *4:1–13*
   D. Acknowledging a gift  *4:14–23*

☐ **Overview of Colossians: Focus on Christ**
Colosse was a minor city in the Roman province of Asia (now Turkey) situated about 100 miles east of Ephesus on the main trade route. Paul had never visited Colosse but had received a report on the church there from Epaphras, who was probably responsible for bringing the gospel to that city.

Paul's main reason for writing was to dismantle what some scholars call "the Colossian heresy," a peculiar blend of false teaching which included Greek and Jewish elements. From the Greeks came some early form of gnosticism (which didn't become widespread until the second century). This heresy reduced Jesus to just one of many beings which had emanated from God. With this came the idea that some special "insiders'" knowledge was required to truly understand Christianity. From Judaism was added some forms of legalism, the keeping of various parts of the Jewish law, such as circumcision, in addition to having faith in Christ.

Paul masterfully handles this odd heresy and does so in a positive and encouraging way. Throughout the letter our attention is drawn to Jesus Christ; this focus on Christ is the best way to correct error and find direction for Christian living.

**Outline of Colossians**
I. Correction for Error
   A. Thanksgiving and prayer  *1:1–14*
   B. Description of Christ  *1:15–23*
   C. Paul's situation  *1:24–2:7*
   D. Erasing errors  *2:8–3:14*
II. Directions for Living
   A. Old and new habits  *3:5–17*
   B. Christian households  *3:18–4:1*
   C. Instructions and greetings  *4:2–18*

# 1/Galatians 1:1-2:21
# Personal Defense

□ **Introduction**

*Ad hominem* is a Latin phrase which literally means "to the man." The phrase is often used to describe a kind of argument which uses an attack on the person involved rather than employing facts and reason to win the argument.

For example, a Christian and an atheist are discussing the existence of God.

"There is no way you can prove to me there is a God," the atheist declares. "He's just part of the world's collective imagination. People have always wished for a kind of superman to help them with their problems, so they have imagined that there is a God. But the fact is, everywhere you look there are problems, sickness, war, and suffering. God can't help people with these problems because he just isn't there. And even if he were, there would be no way to get through to him."

"Those are difficult issues you raise," the Christian responds, "but I think you will understand God better if you consider Jesus Christ. You see, the most significant thing about Jesus is that he claimed to be God. And a fair evaluation of the evidence makes it hard to believe he was wrong. If you want to know God you should look at Jesus Christ."

"That's the problem with you Christians!" the atheist explodes, "you are so gullible. You believe anything. I say you're all a bunch of negative, archaic, super-stitious fanatics. Not only that, you're ignorant and you don't face the facts. There's just no way you can prove to me that there is a God."

This is an argument *ad hominem*. Instead of logically responding to the points raised by the Christian in the discussion, the atheist launched a personal attack on the Christian in an effort to win the argument.

The apostle Paul encountered this sort of *ad hominem* tactic from the false teachers in Galatia. While Paul was out of town, these teachers had begun to preach a different, modified gospel (1:6).

One of the ways they had attempted to gain acceptance for their ideas was by attacking Paul's personal credentials. Nowhere does Paul specifically list these accusations. But by what he writes in response to them, we get a pretty good picture of what they were.

The false teachers said Paul wasn't *really* an apostle, since he wasn't one of the original Twelve. They insinuated that he had no authority to preach the gospel he did. They implied that Paul was some sort of demagogue, merely trying to win public favor.

You will find these first four readings filled with information about Paul's personal history. He explains how he was converted and how he received the gospel he preached (1:11–17). He reports what he did after his conversion and even shares the details of a touchy confrontation he had with Peter.

Paul uses these facts about his own life to rebut the gossipy accusations of his detractors in Galatia. As you will see, the first part of Paul's letter is intended to kick the legs out from under the troublesome *ad hominem* attacks of the false teachers. It is Paul's personal defense.

An interesting sidelight in these readings is the apostle's tone. To put it bluntly, he is boiling mad. He's so angry at the false teachers that twice he seems to shout at the one responsible for the personal attacks, "Let him be eternally condemned!" (1:8–9).

This raises some questions about anger. When is it appropriate for a Christian to get angry? When is it not? As you work through these studies, look closely at Paul's personal defense, but also see if you can formulate an answer to this question: "Are there situations around me about which God is angry and I am not?"

☐ **Key Verse 1: Galatians 2:20**
I have been crucified with Christ and I no longer live, but Christ lives in me. The life I live in the body, I live by faith in the Son of God, who loved me and gave himself for me.

☐ **Outline**

*Galatians: Defending the Gospel*

**I.  Personal Defense**
**A. Greeting and purpose for writing   *1:1-10***
**B. Paul's gospel explained   *1:11-24***
**C. Paul's gospel tested   *2:1-21***

II.  Theological Defense
A. Abraham and God   *3:1-14*
B. Law and faith   *3:15-4:31*

III. Moral Defense
A. Freedom in Christ   *5:1-26*
1. Don't lose it   *1-12*
2. Don't abuse it   *13-26*
B. Final instructions   *6:1-18*

# 1

☐ **PRAY for insight into God's Word**
Lord, I thank you for your servant, Paul. Please give me a fresh understanding of what he wrote, and why.

☐ **READ Galatians 1:1–10**

☐ **MEDITATE on God's Word**

*Discovery*
**1.** Right from the start of his letter, what question is Paul answering (1–2, 6–9)? What seems to be his purpose for writing?

_____

_____

**2.** What does the phrase "deliver us" (RSV, KJV, NASB) or "rescue us" (NEB, NIV) in verse 4 teach you about the nature of salvation? What other facts about salvation do you find in verses 1–5?

_____

_____

_____

**3.** What is the most serious consequence of accepting a different gospel (6)? How does Paul react toward those who teach it?

_____

_____

*Note: different gospel (6)—"The false teachers were evidently Judaizers, whose 'gospel' is summarized in Acts 15:1. They did not believe that you must believe in Jesus for salvation, but they stressed that you must be circumcised and keep the law as well. In other words, you must let Moses finish what Christ has begun. Or rather, you yourself must finish, by your obedience to the law, what Christ has begun. You must add your works to the work of Christ. You must finish Christ's unfinished work" (John R. W. Stott, Only One Way, The Bible Speaks Today Series [InterVarsity Press, 1968], p. 22).*

**4.** Finish this statement according to your own understanding, "The true gospel is . . ."

_____

_____

_____

### Reflection

Usually when Paul wrote to a first-century church, he would begin with a warm greeting followed by words of praise and encouragement—but not in his letter to the Galatians. Instead, he immediately "comes out swinging."

The gospel was being viciously attacked in Galatia so Paul launches his counter-attack on two fronts.

*Paul's place and authority as an apostle.* This was questioned by Judaizing Jewish Christians—hence the statements in verses 1, 8, 10. Note how he replies:

—He received his authority directly from God—human "ordination" is irrelevant (1).

—He is absolutely certain that what he preached is the truth (8).

—What men think of him is of no consequence (10).

*The purity and truth of the gospel.* Verse 4 refers to two key themes of the whole epistle—forgiveness and freedom, which are Christ's work and God's will. Note the special emphasis on the unity of "God the Father and our Lord Jesus Christ" in this opening paragraph. Was this because Jewish legalism was an incipient denial of Christ's unique status and full equality with God? It is significant that the Jehovah's Witnesses deny Christ's deity and impose a strict set of rules and regulations on members. Legalism, in any form, always involves a reduction of Christ's authority and glory.

### My Response

### Memory Point

Write out Key Verse 1 (Gal. 2:20) on a 3x5 card and place it in a familiar spot. Whenever you see it throughout the day, say the verse aloud several times. On the last page of this book all Key Verses are printed from the *New International Version*; there is also space to copy the verses from another version, if you wish.

### ☐ PRAY to apply God's Word

Thank God for the people he used to communicate the gospel to you . . .

# 2

☐ **PRAY for insight into God's Word**
"Speak Lord, for your servant is listening" (1 Sam. 3:9 NIV).

☐ **READ Galatians 1:11-24**

☐ **MEDITATE on God's Word**

*Discovery*
**1.** How did Paul learn the gospel he preached (12)? What accusation would such a fact answer?

_____

_____

**2.** What was Paul's original goal in life (13-14)? What had motivated him (13-14)?

_____

_____

_____

**3.** What new life goal did he adopt (16b)? What caused the switch (15-16)?

_____

_____

_____

**4.** Briefly state your own goal in life. How has knowing Jesus affected your life goal? How else could or should it?

_____

_____

_____

_____

## Reflection

Paul shared a bit of his personal history with the Galatians and, in particular, he focused on how the gospel had affected his life, and in so doing, he underscored his apostolic authority. Paul stated that the gospel was:

*Revealed to him (11-12).* Its startling message of deliverance from sin (4) and justification by faith in Christ (2:20) was mediated to him not by any human agency but by divine revelation. We may be spiritually indebted to preachers, teachers, personal evangelists, and parents, but we ought to share Paul's conviction that we understand the gospel only because God has revealed himself to us (1 Cor. 1:18; 2:10, 14).

*Effective in him (13-14).* It was not only a truth that appealed to Paul's mind, but a message that transformed his religiously zealous (14) but spiritually barren life. Saul the adversary became Paul the advocate. Through grace (15) he was called to Christ, though long before that moment he had been "set apart" in God's purpose for an evangelistic ministry of immense power and effectiveness.

*Proclaimed by him (15-23).* All this was a revelation to Paul (12, 16), but he soon realized it was given to him that he might share it with others (16). Paul wisely spent a long time meditating on these great truths (17-18). Do we give ourselves to serious study of the Bible and Christian doctrine so that we are deeply persuaded about what we believe? Do we consider how we can best communicate the gospel to our desperately needy contemporaries?

## My Response

## Memory Point

Review Key Verse 1 (Gal. 2:20) until you can say it three times in a row without a mistake. Try to have someone check you.

## ☐ PRAY to apply God's Word

"Teach us, good Lord, to serve thee as thou deservest; to give and not to count the cost; to fight and not to heed the wounds; to toil and not to ask for rest; to labor and not to ask for any reward save knowing that we do thy will. Through Jesus Christ our Lord" *Ignatius of Loyola.*

# 3

☐ **PRAY for insight into God's Word**
"The law of the LORD is perfect, reviving the soul. The statutes of the LORD are trustworthy, making wise the simple (Ps. 19:7).

☐ **READ Galatians 2:1-10**

☐ **MEDITATE on God's Word**

*Discovery*
**1.** Why did Paul go to Jerusalem (2)? Of what significance was it that he brought Titus (3)?

_____

_____

**2.** What were the results of the Jerusalem visit (3-9)? What advice was Paul given (10)?

_____

_____

_____

**3.** What form of opposition did Paul encounter during his visit (4)? Why might these people have been afraid to let the gospel spread to the Gentiles?

_____

_____

_____

**4.** In your discussion about Christianity with others, on what issues should you take an attitude similar to Paul's (5)? When is compromise appropriate?

_____

_____

_____

## Reflection

Although Paul was hotly defending issues that went to the very heart of the gospel, we see in today's reading that he never lost his balanced perspective—he knew when to be dogmatic and when to be flexible.

*Paul's intolerance.* "False brothers" (4) were always a source of trouble to Paul. Because they had not experienced the freedom from legalism that Christ had won, they tried to bring others back into bondage (4); but they met their match in Paul. Holding firm to the fact that Titus, a Greek with two Gentile parents, had not been forced to be circumcised (3), Paul refused to submit to other Judaistic rulings. This "me against the world" attitude, however, was not based on professional jealousy or a lust for power in the Christian hierarchy. "The truth of the gospel" was at stake (5), and for *that* Paul was prepared to "go it alone."

*Paul's reasonableness.* Paul did not enjoy his isolation. He was sure of the stand he was making, yet longed that others would see things his way. He wanted support, and was prepared to check his ideas with those who had found Christ before him. He had a healthy fear of "running in vain" (2). And so he discussed matters with other Christian leaders. The results were very positive: the apostles recognized that Paul had received grace (9), they agreed on a profitable division of missionary labor (7), and they made a helpful suggestion which he already was eager to follow (10). Christians today should be able to resolve differences of opinion in a similar way, with mutual love and toleration.

## My Response

## Memory Point

Try to put Key Verse 1 (Gal. 2:20) to music (create your own tune or use an existing one). Then sing or whistle your verse throughout the day.

## ☐ PRAY to apply God's Word

Pray about one area where you need to become more dogmatic and one area where you need to be more flexible . . .

# 4

□ **PRAY for insight into God's Word**

"O Father, comfort and strengthen me, a poor, suffering man, with thy holy Word. I cannot endure thy hand, yet I shall be condemned if I do not endure it. So strengthen me, Father, that I may not despair. Amen" *(Martin Luther)*.

□ **READ Galatians 2:11-21**

□ **MEDITATE on God's Word**

*Discovery*

**1.** Why did Paul confront Peter in public (11-14)? Why was Peter's cowardly behavior especially odd (see Acts 10:1—11:18)?

_____

_____

**2.** What groups or ideas *within the church* today pressure us to alter the gospel? How and when does God want you to confront these groups or ideas?

_____

_____

**3.** In Paul's day, how were people attempting to be "justified by works of the law" (16)? In what ways are people caught up with the same struggle today? Are you ever one of these?

_____

_____

_____

_____

**4.** To what extent is verse 20 true of you? What is the evidence? What actions and attitudes of yours need to be subjected to Christ's lordship in your life?

_____

_____

_____

_____

## Reflection

In the closing section of Paul's personal defense, we find three statements beginning with the pronoun "I." They show us what a deep and clear understanding of the gospel Paul had.

*"I opposed Cephas to his face" (11).* Paul was now the only strong personality in the infant church. Peter, too, had made his presence felt, but the same fear of people that had once caused him to deny Christ had led him to deny the unity between Jew and Gentile that Christ died to win (see Eph. 2:11-16). Having formerly mixed freely with Gentile Christians, he had retreated to the safety of segregation, influencing even the tolerant Barnabas by his attitude (13). Paul took him to task for this "in front of them all" (14). Ignoring a real difference of opinion on an important Christian issue, as Peter had done, may prove to be not diplomatic tact but a denial of the truth of the gospel (14).

*"I do not set aside the grace of God" (21).* Either the Christian or the non-Christian can try to do this, by trying to "balance" guilt with good works, or by insisting on carrying the load of guilt himself. We must put it down where it belongs: at the Cross of Christ.

*"I live by faith in the Son of God" (20).* Paul had been "killed" spiritually by the kind of allegiance to the law that Peter was defending. The driving force in the new life given to him by Christ was not a law, an ideal, or a system, but a Person. Secure in a love that had proved itself in death, he was now free to live with complete confidence in Christ.

## My Response

## Memory Point

How could you use Key Verse 1 (Gal. 2:20) in a witnessing situation?

## ☐ PRAY to apply God's Word

Pray for one person you know who is familiar with the gospel but who does not understand it. Ask God to use you to communicate the truth of the gospel to that person . . .

# 2/Galatians 3:1–4:31
# Theological Defense

## ☐ Introduction

It was during World War I that a young man developed a conviction which helped him become one of the most influential Christian authors of the twentieth century. "Ever since I served as an infantryman in the first world war," C. S. Lewis wrote in the preface to *Mere Christianity*, "I have had a great dislike of people who, themselves in ease and safety, issue exhortations to men in the front line. As a result I have a reluctance to say much about temptations to which I myself am not exposed."

Many years later, as he wrote his autobiography, *Surprised by Joy*, Lewis still clung to the same conviction. "I will not indulge in futile philippics against enemies I have never met in battle."

The temptation Lewis felt most deeply was the temptation to be his own god. The battle he had fought the hardest was that of a rebelliously independent unbeliever struggling to resist a loving Savior. So after his conversion he became an effective communicator of the gospel to "hard-boiled atheists."

The apostle Paul had a similar situation. Before his conversion to Christianity, he was a zealous Jew, having become an expert in the Law and the history of Israel as he studied under the great Hebrew teacher Gamaliel. As a Pharisee, he was given the official duty of eliminating any Jew who believed in Jesus Christ.

Since Paul, like C. S. Lewis, "had been behind enemy lines" before his conversion, he was able to turn back the arguments of his contemporaries. We will see this clearly in our next five readings.

The false teachers in Galatia were waging a theological attack on Christianity. They were claiming that to be fully Christian a person must believe in Jesus *and* become a good Jew, by being circumcised and following the Law.

Because of his own background as a Pharisee, Paul fully understood the mind of the Judaizers and why they clung so doggedly to Judaism. So in Galatians chapters 3 and 4 Paul said to these false teachers, "OK, I understand why you still think Judaism is superior to faith in Jesus Christ, but I'm going to show you *from your own Scriptures*, why you are wrong."

First, he explained how Abraham, the father of Judaism, had pleased God through faith rather than through keeping the law. Upholding that precedent was devastating to the arguments of the Judaizers.

Having established the principle of justification by faith, Paul proceeded to show how it interprets God's covenant with Abraham and the true function of the law. Paul concluded with a complex allegory of two women and two covenants. It was Paul's theological knockout punch, as if he were saying, "See, I can take your best evidence and prove you are wrong from it." He was able to outwit the Judaizers on their own turf.

Don't be discouraged if you have trouble following all of Paul's points. It will help you to review the appropriate Old Testament passages if you have time. But do make sure you reflect on the overall message of these chapters: that God planned the entire history of Israel so that you too would have an opportunity to enter the kingdom of God.

## ☐ Key Verse 2: Galatians 4:4-6

But when the time had fully come, God sent his Son, born of a woman, born under law, to redeem those under law, that we might receive the full rights of sons. Because you are sons, God sent the Spirit of his Son into our hearts, the Spirit who calls out, "*Abba*, Father."

## ☐ Outline

### *Galatians: Defending the Gospel*

1. Personal Defense
   A. Greeting and purpose for writing   *1:1-10*
   B. Paul's gospel explained   *1:11-24*
   C. Paul's gospel tested   *2:1-21*

II. **Theological Defense**
   A. **Abraham and God**   *3:1-14*
   B. **Law and faith**   *3:15-4:31*

III. Moral Defense
   A. Freedom in Christ   *5:1-26*
      1. Don't lose it   *1-12*
      2. Don't abuse it   *13-26*
   B. Final instructions   *6:1-18*

# 5

☐ **PRAY for insight into God's Word**
Lord Jesus, I ask you to give me a clearer, deeper understanding of what faith in you is through what I am about to read and study.

☐ **READ Galatians 3:10–14**

☐ **MEDITATE on God's Word**

*Discovery*
**1.** What is Paul's main point about the law (10–14)?

_____

_____

_____

**2.** What are some ways the word "redeemed" is used in everyday life today? What insight does that give you into Paul's use of the word (13–14)? How does it explain *your* salvation?

_____

_____

_____

**3.** What is your responsibility to persons *in your church* who say, "It doesn't really matter what religion you have; what God cares about is whether you live a good life or not"?

_____

_____

_____

**4.** What causes you to continue putting your faith in Jesus? What makes that faith real to you?

_____

_____

_____

### Reflection

People always seem to think that as long as they do their best they will be all right with God. They think that they can *earn* their salvation. These teachers who had so confused the Galatians were just like that. They believed that keeping the law was the only thing that mattered. Paul showed how wrong such thinking was and is.

*Acceptance by God has nothing to do with our efforts.* If that *were* the case, each and every law would have to be kept. Obviously that is impossible, so those who rely on the law are condemned by it. They can never satisfy God's standards (10).

*Acceptance by God has nothing to do with nationality.* The "legalists" relied on their descent from Abraham as well as their keeping of the law. Paul pointed out that the true descendant of Abraham is the person who lives by faith. It is not a physical matter. Living in a "Christian" country, or having Christian parents, doesn't automatically make us Christians.

*Acceptance by God is only by faith.* Christ made this possible and we depend entirely on him. All the things that we could not do he has done. He has taken the punishment that belonged to us for breaking the law (11-13).

### My Response

### Memory Point

Write out your own paraphrase of Key Verse 2 (Gal. 4:4-6).

### □ PRAY to apply God's Word

Pray for someone you know who works hard to live a good life but who still needs to accept Jesus Christ as Savior . . .

# 6

☐ PRAY for insight into God's Word
Sing a hymn or chorus of praise to begin your time with God (or hum it to yourself). As you do, close your eyes and imagine yourself standing before his throne singing to him alone.

☐ READ Galatians 3:1-9

☐ MEDITATE on God's Word

*Discovery*
**1.** What was it about the Galatian Christians that exasperated Paul (1–5)?

_____

_____

**2.** Why do you think it was so clever and important for Paul to link Abraham with the principle of faith (6–9)?

_____

_____

*Note: Consider Abraham (6)—"To a Jew the authority of Abraham was decisive. Paul shows that, theologically, Abraham was accepted by God through faith, not works. Scripture thus corroborates Paul's gospel and their own experience" (Samuel J. Mikolaski, The New Bible Commentary: Revised, Galatians [Eerdmans, 1970], p. 1097).*

**3.** Are there ways you are tempted to rely more on "human effort" (3) than on faith as your approach to God? If so, how? When and in what sense is human effort good and proper?

_____

_____

_____

**4.** In what area of your life do you need to exercise more faith? What would it mean for you to do that this week?

_____

_____

_____

### Reflection

In Paul's defense of the gospel, he began to employ a slightly different tactic; he switched from an argument rooted in personal experience (chapters 1–2) to one rooted in theology and the Old Testament. His cry in verse 1 was one of bewilderment (see also 1:6) at the Galatians' failure to interpret correctly three important factors:

*Paul's preaching (1).* The Christ presented to them was a crucified Savior. Why should Christ have bothered to die if men could save themselves by keeping the law?

*Their own experience (2–5).* Their past reception of the Spirit (2), here synonymous with conversion, and his current working among them were all dependent on faith.

*The Old Testament Scriptures (6–9).* The Jewish Christians would have regarded Abraham very highly. But he was accepted by God not because he kept the law but because of his faith.

This doesn't mean that laws aren't important. They are and without them society would grind to a halt. Some of the laws God revealed to Moses were for all people for all time. Others were designed to prepare the way for Jesus. As Christians, our lives should reflect something of God's character and so we will want to keep his laws. The fact is, though, that no amount of law keeping, church going, self-denial or hard work will put us right with God. Only Jesus can. And that's why our faith in him is paramount.

### My Response

### Memory Point

Write out Key Verse 2 (Gal. 4:4–6) on a 3x5 card and place it in a familiar spot. Whenever you see it throughout the day repeat it several times.

### ☐ PRAY to apply God's Word

Consult your answer to question 4 on the previous page. Pray about the area in which you are most in need of faith. Ask the Holy Spirit to help you do something about it this week . . .

# 7

☐ **PRAY for insight into God's Word**
Lord, I need a word from you today. Please speak to me through what I am about to read.

☐ **READ Galatians 3:15–29**

☐ **MEDITATE on God's Word**

*Discovery*
**1.** What truth about God does the example in verse 15 express?

_____

**2.** Explain the distinction Paul makes between "offspring" or "seed" and "off-springs" or "seeds" (16). Why is it important that we belong to Christ (29)?

_____

_____

_____

**3.** What is the significance of the law for you? How do you think the Old Testament applies to you today?

_____

_____

_____

**4.** In what sense are we "all one in Christ Jesus" (28)? In what specific way has this truth affected your thinking? Your words? Your actions?

_____

_____

_____

### Reflection

These verses almost seem like a duel. Paul's weapon is faith; the Judaizers wield the Law. As the "action" progresses, we watch Paul make three devastating jabs.

*Faith is not superseded by law (15–18).* The law, the Jewish Christians claim, had come after the promise to Abraham, and so had annulled it. Not at all, Paul says. The promise was like a will, and could not be set aside (17).

*The law is not able to give life (19–22).* The law has its function—it shows up sin for what it is. Like the double yellow line down the center of the highway, it makes error obvious. But it cannot correct or deliver us from it.

*The law is superseded by faith (23–29).* Paul turns the Jewish argument back on his attackers. If we are going to be guided by the order of events in time, faith is God's last word—spoken in and through Christ. He did not call men to be saved by obeying the law; he opened up a new way to God, the way of faith in his sacrifice on the cross.

Verse 23 suggests a picture of the law as a harsh prison warden. Paul balances this by introducing the idea of a "custodian," or someone "put in charge to lead us to Christ" (24–25). But grown-up children no longer need such "supervision" (25). If we have "put on" or "been clothed with" Christ, we have entered a new order in which race distinctions (Jew or Greek), class distinctions (slave or free), and sex distinctions (male or female) are of no consequence.

### My Response

### Memory Point

Review Key Verse 2 (Gal. 4:4–6) until you can say it three times in a row without making a mistake.

### □ PRAY to apply God's Word

Today, pray for the needs of your church or fellowship group . . .

# 8

☐ **READ Galatians 4:1–11**

☐ **MEDITATE on God's Word**

*Discovery*
**1.** In what sense were the Galatian Christians like children (1–7)? In what ways were they like slaves?

_____

_____

**2.** Verses 4–7 contain the story of salvation. Organize the facts as if for a newspaper story: a. What happened? b. Who was responsible? c. When did it happen? d. Why did it happen? e. Now write a headline for the story.

_____

_____

_____

_____

**3.** What problem does Paul point to in verses 8–11? What did this reveal about his readers?

_____

_____

**4.** In what ways are you tempted to think or act as you did before you became a Christian? What precautions could you take now to squash these temptations before they come?

_____

_____

_____

### Reflection

Paul uses two illustrations of change to underline the freedom that Christ can bring to a life: childhood to maturity (1-2) and slavery to sonship (4-7).

In this context he means slavery to the "elemental spirits of the universe" or the "basic principles of the world" (3). Paul implies that the effect on the Galatians was spiritual poverty, for these spirits or principles were "weak and miserable" (9). It is sadly possible for any Christian to continue living in the "hovel" of a pre-Christian lifestyle, and it is just as illogical today as it was for Paul's readers (9b). The regulations which bind us may not be "days, months, seasons, years" (10), but the bondage may be just as crippling.

Freedom, however, does not mean independence. The mature Christian still recognizes the need and privilege of calling God "Abba! Father!" (6). Humanity (Christian or otherwise) has not "come of age" in the sense that we can live outside the scope of God's fatherly care. And sonship does not mean presumption. The initiative for adoption into God's family was taken by God himself (4-5). God's adoption process began in Christ "when the time had fully come" (4). His timing for action is always exactly right.

### My Response

### Memory Point

Go back and review Key Verse 1 (Gal. 2:20). Then, without looking, say both Key Verse 1 (Gal. 2:20) and Key Verse 2 (Gal. 4:4-6).

### ☐ PRAY to apply God's Word

Ask your heavenly Father to help you understand how being a son or daughter of God should alter your actions today . . .

# 9

☐ **PRAY** for insight into God's Word
Quiet yourself before the living God by closing your eyes and meditating as you breathe. Each time you exhale imagine you are giving up a concern or worry to God. Each time you inhale, imagine you are being filled with his Spirit for study and service.

☐ **READ Galatians 4:12-20**

☐ **MEDITATE on God's Word**

*Discovery*
**1.** In what sense would Paul want his readers to become like himself (12)? How had he become like them?

_____

_____

*Note: become like me, for I became like you (12)—This "opening clause is a puzzle. Literally it reads, 'Be like me, as I too (have become) like you.' NEB is probably right in turning it, 'Put yourselves in my place . . . for I have put myself in yours.' On the other hand, he may simply mean, 'Be as frank and loving with me as I have always been with you.' Either way, it is clearly a personal appeal to the Galatians to resume their old friendly terms with Paul which have apparently been ruptured by the work of the Judaizers" (Alan Cole, The Epistle of Paul to the Galatians, The Tyndale New Testament Commentary [Eerdmans, 1965], pp. 120-121).*

**2.** What clues do you pick up about the apostle's physical condition (12-15); see also 6:11 and 2 Cor. 12:7-10)? Do you let appearances influence your opinions of people in your church? How? Why?

_____

_____

_____

**3.** What specific accusation from the Judaizers does Paul seem to be addressing in verses 13-20?

_____

_____

**4.** Looking back over the last year, try to identify some evidence that Christ is being formed in you (19).

_____

_____

## Reflection

Right in the middle of this argument, carefully based on Scripture and theological thought, Paul appeals to past happy experience and to warm personal relationships. Often impersonal and purely academic theological debate hardens attitudes and divides Christian brothers and sisters; it is good to ask ourselves periodically if that is happening *to us*. Creating divisions is the work of the enemies of Christ (17).

*A plea from history (12-15).* Fascinating but baffling glimpses of Paul's ministry and physical needs are given us here. Something about his health had caused them difficulties (14); commentators have speculated about epilepsy, an eye disease or other maladies without knowing exactly what it was. But the Galatians had overwhelmed him with their warm welcome and loving acceptance. How could they have changed so greatly? But apparently they had—and Christians today can do the same, unfortunately!

*A plea from the heart (16-20).*
—An apostle's concern—"I am again in the pains of childbirth" (19). The "again" refers back to Paul's first evangelistic mission in Galatia. He was no mere itinerant evangelist, holding meetings and moving on; for him it was as profound and costly an experience as child-bearing, and he gave everything to it.
—An apostle's aim—"Until Christ is formed in you" (19). Note how the metaphor of childbirth is used to illustrate the continued cost to the Christian worker of furthering God's purposes for his converts, and the ultimate goal of the life-giving process: "Christ formed in you."

## My Response

## Memory Point

Whenever you look at your watch or a clock today, say Key Verse 2 (Gal. 4:4-6).

## ☐ PRAY to apply God's Word

Tell God you want to become more like Christ; then talk to him about the areas you need help in doing so . . .

# *10*

☐ **PRAY for insight into God's Word**
Thank God for three things; then ask him to bless your study of his Word today.

☐ **READ Galatians 4:21–31**

☐ **MEDITATE on God's Word**

*Discovery*
**1.** Who is Paul challenging in these verses (21)? Where does Paul get "ammunition" for his counterattack (21b)?

_____

_____

**2.** If your time permits, read the background to Paul's reference to Sarah and Hagar in Genesis 16, 17 and 21. Summarize by jotting down the significant details of that story here.

_____

_____

_____

_____

_____

**3.** What point is Paul making by unfolding this portion of Jewish history (24–31)?

_____

_____

_____

_____

**4.** What does the word "covenant" (24) teach you about the way God deals with mankind?

_____

_____

### Reflection

In this fascinating passage, Paul uses some incidents in Genesis as an allegory. This way of interpreting the Scriptures was commonly used in his day, especially in the rabbinic schools, and was therefore familiar to his readers. The passage is clearly addressed to those readers who want to be "under the law" (21)—Christian believers who had returned to a form of "salvation-by-works" teaching. The apostle illustrates his theme by drawing a sharp, contrasting picture between old- and new-covenant children, between the children of slavery and the children of promise.

*Children of slavery (24).* The legalists, who insisted on ceremonial observance or specific cultic acts as a means of securing their salvation, are here likened to Hagar's offspring. They are the children of a slave and will always be in bondage to the law. They are born "in the ordinary way" (29), and are the persecutors (29) who are rejected (30).

*Children of promise (28).* The apostle now contrasts those who rely upon the works of the law with those who depend upon the truth of the promise (23). The legalists are part of the earthly Jerusalem (25), but believers who trust the promise are part of the heavenly Jerusalem (26). They received the promised inheritance (30), for the Holy Spirit is responsible for their spiritual birth (29).

### My Response

### Memory Point

What makes Key Verse 2 (Gal. 4:4-6) meaningful to you?

### ☐ PRAY to apply God's Word

Pray about one way you are still a "slave" and ask the Holy Spirit to give you freedom . . .

# 3/Galatians 5:1-6:18
# Moral Defense

## ☐ Introduction

Leaving home is an essential step in the process of a young person's maturation. Some leave to enter college, others to get married or to get a job and an apartment. Still others leave home to join the armed forces.

Yet leaving home often turns out to be a painful experience because it produces a new kind of relationship between parents and child. And it is so easy at first for this new relationship to become unbalanced.

For instance, a son, once freed from what he thinks are confining parental regulations, is tempted to overindulge in things that were once forbidden. He may expose himself to harmful influences, either intellectual or spiritual. He may choose bad friends, waste his money, develop a destructive habit, or join an unhealthy group. Freedom from parental guidance has a way of luring some young men into dangerous excess.

On the other hand, parents can upset the new relationship with their son by not letting go. A mother may attempt to get her son to marry the kind of girl she thinks is best. A father may pressure his son to excell in a career the son doesn't really like. Both parents may subtly withhold their love from a son who does not follow their blueprint for his life.

As a young boy, the son had a profound need for the rules his parents imposed. But when he leaves home he must learn to live a responsible, productive, godly life, not because he is forced to, but because he wants to. This is exactly the sort of message Paul has for his readers in chapters 5 and 6 of Galatians where he is attempting to explain the balanced nature of the freedom believers have in Christ.

Because of their faith in Jesus Christ, the Galatians were free from the bondage of keeping all the picky details of the Jewish law in order to receive salvation. But, like parents who are unable to let go of a son, some of the Galatians were trying to reimpose the Jewish Law on Christians. To this extreme Paul says, "do not let yourselves be burdened again by the yoke of slavery" (5:1).

On the other hand, like the son who pursues unhealthy excess, some of the Galatians were abusing their new freedom in Christ. "If Christ has set us free," they reasoned, "we can do as we please." But Paul squashes that error by quickly adding, "do not use your freedom to indulge the sinful nature" (5:13).

In these final studies in Galatians you will discover Paul's moral defense of Christianity by examining his definition of Christian freedom. Paul says we will know we have truly understood the nature of this new Christian freedom when we see the fruits of the Spirit in our lives: love, joy, peace, patience, kindness, goodness, faithfulness, gentleness and self-control. In other words, when we practice these things not because we have to, but because we want to, then we have discovered the secret of freedom in Christ.

□ **Key Verse 3: Galatians 5:22-23**

But the fruit of the Spirit is love, joy, peace, patience, kindness, goodness, faithfulness, gentleness and self-control. Against such things there is no law.

□ **Outline**

*Galatians: Defending the Gospel*

I. Personal Defense
   A. Greeting and purpose for writing  *1:1-10*
   B. Paul's gospel explained  *1:11-24*
   C. Paul's gospel tested  *2:1-21*

II. Theological Defense
   A. Abraham and God  *3:1-14*
   B. Law and faith  *3:15-4:31*

III. **Moral Defense**
   A. **Freedom in Christ**  *5:1-26*
      1. **Don't lose it**  *1-12*
      2. **Don't abuse it**  *13-26*
   B. **Final instructions**  *6:1-18*

# 11

□ **PRAY for insight into God's word**
"The ordinances of the Lord are . . . more precious than gold . . . they are sweeter than honey . . . By them is your servant warned; in keeping them there is great reward" (Ps. 19:9–11).

□ **READ Galatians 5:1-12**

□ **MEDITATE on God's Word**

*Discovery*
**1.** What had Christ set the Galatians (and us) free from (1)? What, then, is the significance of Paul's terse command "stand firm" (1)? In what sense are Christians free?

_____

_____

_____

**2.** In Paul's opinion, what would agreeing to be circumcised indicate about the Galatians (3-4)?

_____

_____

*Note: A little yeast works through the whole batch of dough (9)—"A small portion of legalism, if it be mixed with the gospel, corrupts its purity. To add legal ordinances and works in the least degree to justification by faith, is to undermine the whole" (Robert Jamieson, A. R. Fausset, and David Brown, Commentary on the Whole Bible [Grand Rapids: Zondervan, 1961], p. 1274).*

**3.** In what ways do twentieth-century Christians give in to legalism? What outward things do we substitute for a true and living walk with God?

_____

_____

_____

**4.** How are you most susceptible to being caught up in legalism? What one thing could you do (or not do) this month to counter a legalistic tendency in yourself?

_____

_____

_____

## Reflection

In these verses, it seems that Paul turns from his attackers to the Galatian Christians themselves and says, "How *could* you swallow such a lie? Can't you see the difference between the law and faith yet?" He uses two phrases to explain the difference once again.

*"For freedom Christ has set us free" (1).* Christians are adopted sons, not slaves, and God does not want his sons to behave like slaves. For the Galatian Christians, exposed to the arguments of the Judaizers, bondage consisted partly in never being quite sure whether they had kept all the rules satisfactorily (3). For modern Christians there may be several variations on that theme, but the possibilities are the same: either a total acceptance of grace, or a total subjection to law.

*"You have fallen away from grace" (45).* Although the grace of Christ continually flows out towards the Christian, and always seeks to reach him, any Christian may put himself in a position where he can no longer enjoy that grace. "He who disbelieves [the power of grace] can receive no benefit from that which he doubts" (Chrysostom). For such a person Christ will be of no benefit, for, as far as that person is concerned, Christ died to no purpose (3:21). Christ cannot be supplemented without being deposed, and the Christian who tries to make Christ redundant is, temporarily at least, "alienated from Christ" (4).

No wonder Paul reacts so violently against those who tried to bring his Galatian friends into bondage again, and so were confusing (10), agitating (12), and hindering (7) them. In Paul's anger is the true love of the pastor for his people.

## My Response

## Memory Point

Write out Key Verse 3 (Gal. 5:22–23) on a 3x5 card. Take the card with you during the day and practice whenever you have a spare moment.

## ☐ PRAY to apply God's Word

Use a "different than usual" prayer position (stand with your arms raised or kneel, for example) and worship Jesus in your time of prayer today . . .

# 12

☐ **PRAY for insight into God's Word**

"Jesus, the very thought of thee with sweetness fills the breast; but sweeter far thy face to see, and in thy presence rest" *(Bernard of Clairvaux).*

☐ **READ Galatians 5:13-26**

☐ **MEDITATE on God's Word**

*Discovery*

**1.** According to Paul, how are we to guard against abusing our freedom in Christ (13-15)? Give one example of how you've seen this safeguard working in your life.

_____

_____

**2.** What dichotomy does Paul point out in verses 16 and 17? Do you agree with him? Why or why not?

_____

_____

_____

**3.** Which of the things listed in verses 22 and 23 are you best at? What new way could you show it to others this week? Which one are you worst at? How could you improve it this week?

_____

_____

_____

**4.** In what ways has the Holy Spirit actively shaped your life in the last year? Jot down the areas that you need his help to change in the coming year.

_____

_____

_____

### Reflection

Today the apostle covers himself against an "attack from the rear." He has been fighting for freedom in Christ but realizes he must explain exactly what that means.

Freedom means love, not license. Paul had dealt with those who think that the way of peace is obedience to the law; now he confronts those who would accept no control at all. Verses 19–21 and 26 give examples of attitudes and actions that presumably characterized some of the Galatian Christians.

A total absence of limits is a perversion of what freedom really is. Sadly, it is a perversion the Western world now proclaims as a virtue. As G. Campbell Morgan wrote, "A room is not a room that has no walls; so liberty is not liberty that has no boundaries."

Later, in Romans 6, Paul will argue that freedom from law observance should lead the Christian to holiness. Sin will not have dominion over us precisely because we are not under the law but under grace (Rom. 6:14). The same result should issue from our living, being led, and keeping in step with the Spirit (16, 18, 25).

The controversy over circumcision had obviously caused damaged relationships that needed to be healed—you bite and devour each other (15). But Paul, as he does so often, accentuates the positive: "serve one another in love" (13). Ministering to, and accepting the ministry of others leaves little time or energy for malicious backbiting.

Paul is both a realist and a positive thinker on the subject of the conflict between the flesh (selfishly motivated desires) and the Spirit. Christ is the Christian's owner and the One for whom he should die daily to sin (24).

### My Response

### Memory Point

Before you go to bed tonight, review Key Verse 3 (Gal. 5:22–23) several times. Also, as soon as you get up the next morning, face yourself in a mirror and say the verse again.

### ☐ PRAY to apply God's Word

Think of the situation where it is most difficult for you to be loving. Talk to God about it and ask him to help you the next time he places you in that situation . . .

# 13

☐ **PRAY for insight into God's Word**
Before you begin your study, have a period of confession.

☐ **READ Galatians 6:1–10**

☐ **MEDITATE on God's Word**

*Discovery*
**1.** How should we react when fellow Christians sin (1–2)? By implication, how should we not react?

_____

_____

**2.** What is the difference between "sowing to sinful nature" and "sowing to the Spirit" (7–8)? How can you avoid legalism in making this distinction?

_____

_____

**3.** What does Paul mean by the phrase "doing good" (9–10)? List five practical ways you could do this and a date by which you will attempt each.

_____

_____

_____

_____

_____

**4.** In what creative ways, in addition to financial giving, could you share good things with your pastor (6)? What are his needs? What would encourage him?

_____

_____

### Reflection

In these verses, Paul shows us another vital aspect of true freedom: responsibility.

*Our responsibility to others.* We must not focus solely on our own development; we must look outward as well. We should do all in our power to restore sinners (1). The fruit of the Spirit (gentleness, 5:23) is immediately put to practical use. We must also carry burdens (2). The legalists impose burdens; Christians bear them for others.

Believers also share gifts (6). Here is a word about our practical support of Christian work. The Christian is eager to "give his teacher a share of all the good things he has" (NEB). And it is not only our money which is to be given, but our time and effort also, for Christians are those who do good (10) to unbelievers as well as to their fellow-Christians.

*Our responsibility to ourselves.* If we are determined to "fulfill the law of Christ" (2) by serving others (5:13), then we must recognize two dangers: temptation (1b) and pride (3). When we come to the aid of those who have fallen we must remember that we, too, can fall (1 Cor. 10:12). We also need to guard against spiritual arrogance (3) as well as self-reliance.

*Our responsibility to God.* All this extremely practical teaching about life in this world is set within the context of eternity (7–8). This future dimension is vital; what we do now determines what we will enjoy then (9).

### My Response

### Memory Point

Whenever you drink anything today, mentally repeat Key Verse 3 (Gal. 5:22–23).

### ☐ PRAY to apply God's Word

Pray for a Christian you know who is "caught in a sin" (1). Ask God if there is any way he wants you to minister to the person . . .

# *14*

☐ **PRAY for insight into God's Word**
Holy Spirit, please use this passage to speak to my circumstances today.

☐ **READ Galatians 6:11–18**

☐ **MEDITATE on God's Word**

*Discovery*
**1.** What rewards were the Judaizers really after (12)? What did they hope to avoid (12)?

_____

_____

**2.** Explain in your own words the effect that the cross had on Paul's priorities in life. Is the same true of you? Why or why not?

_____

_____

**3.** In what ways do you avoid challenge or persecution as a disciple of Christ? Write down one way you feel you *must* stand up for God this year—even if it means opposition.

_____

_____

_____

**4.** What is the most life-changing discovery you have made in your study of Galatians? How have you been acting on that discovery?

_____

_____

_____

_____

### Reflection

Two themes dominate these moving final words, written by Paul himself as he takes the pen from his amanuensis and signs off.

*The Cross of Christ (12, 14, 17).* This is the central glory of Paul's gospel, as it was the controlling principle of his life. The three references are significant; Paul knows what it means to be "persecuted for the Cross," "crucified" by it, and identified so closely with it that his body, too, is marked with Christ's scars. For him the Cross is no pleasant ornament to be hung around the neck; it is nothing less than a way of life—"I die daily," as he once put it. Death in life, as here, and life in death (2 Cor. 4:16)—that is the Christian paradox.

*The Israel of God (16).* The epistle has made it clear that "Israel" now is to be understood not in terms of national descent from Abraham's body, but of spiritual succession to Abraham's faith (see again 3:6–7). The "Israelite" now is the believer in Christ, the "new creation," whether circumcised or uncircumcised (15). He glories, not in the flesh (13)—that is, not in racial descent or physical ceremonies— but in the Cross, by means of which the new international family of God is redeemed and sanctified.

Paul's poignant reminder (17) becomes a final challenge. In what way has knowing Jesus "marked" you so that others can see you are his?

### My Response

### Memory Point

Review Key Verses 1, 2 and 3 (Gal. 2:20; 4:4–6; 5:22–23) until you can say them back to back without an error.

### ☐ PRAY to apply God's Word

"Take my life and let it be consecrated, Lord, to thee. Take my moments and my days, let them flow in ceaseless praise" *Frances R. Havergal.*

# 4/Ephesians 1:1–2:10
## Blessings in Christ

☐ **Introduction**

Take a couple of minutes to review the overview to Ephesians on page 9 before you read the following introduction to the first section of this letter.

A few years ago I had to buy a new car. At that time I decided I wanted to switch to a new company for my auto insurance, so I called them on their 800 telephone line. The operator put me in touch with a crisp, helpful saleswoman and I began to ask my subtle questions.

"What is the minimum amount of insurance I need to satisfy the law in my state?"

She asked me for some basic information about where I lived and what kind of car I was purchasing. I heard her clicking away at a computer keyboard. After a few seconds she was able to give me an exact answer.

"Ah . . . how much will that cost me?" I asked.

Again more clicking and a pause for the computer to spit out the right answer.

"Well, you live in the inner city and that is a high risk area, but still the cost is only $408 for a full year's coverage," she responded. She must have detected that $408 seemed like a lot of money to me, because she began describing the benefits of the policy. "Now of course that includes $30,000 major medical, $10,000 personal injury . . ." On and on she went describing the wonderful coverage her company's auto insurance provided me. Then, being a good salesperson, she pressed me for a decision and I was on the spot. I thought about what I'd rather do with $408. But finally in resignation I replied, "O.K., I'll do it."

I heard feverish clickings on the other end. "Fine, sir. Here is your policy number. You'll need to give it to the dealer when you buy the car. You are covered from this day forward."

A few weeks later I received a fat envelope in the mail with my policy and a letter from the president of the insurance company. He thanked me for choosing his company and explained what my policy was all about. I was glad to receive that letter and written policy, because until I read and studied what the benefits were, I hadn't really understood the full implications of my telephone decision. All I had really known was that I would be $408 poorer in the coming year.

Like the president of my insurance company, the apostle Paul realized the importance of confirming the details of an important decision after it had been made. The Christians in Ephesus had made the most important decision anyone can make. They had decided to turn away from their pagan lifestyle and sins and accept Jesus Christ as Lord and Savior.

But to be sure they fully understood what their decision meant, Paul wrote his Epistle to the Ephesians to fully explain the benefits—"spiritual blessings" (1:3) is the term he used—of being *in Christ*. And there were and still are lots of them.

Paul also knew that the Ephesian Christians were in a high-risk area. Ephesus was a pagan city known for its idol worship and immorality. So he prayed for the Ephesians (1:15–23) and bluntly reminded them of some of the evil influences they were to leave behind as true followers of Christ (2:1–10).

And like the insurance saleswoman who gave me my policy number as a guarantee that I was covered, Paul reminded his readers of the guarantee God had given all who were in Christ—the Holy Spirit. He is the guarantee of our becoming God's own children (1:13–14). And the more we experience of him, the more assured we will be of our own salvation and relationship with God.

As you work your way through these next four studies imagine that you are studying your own insurance policy, because in a sense, that's what it is. The book of Ephesians is God's written confirmation of all the benefits of being in Christ. But, unlike a standard insurance policy, this one is already *paid in full*. God paid for it on your behalf through the death and resurrection of Jesus Christ. And all God asks you to do is accept his gift by faith.

## ☐ Key Verse 4: Ephesians 2:8–10

For it is by grace you have been saved, through faith—and this not from yourselves, it is the gift of God—not by works, so that no one can boast. For we are God's workmanship, created in Christ Jesus to do good works, which God prepared in advance for us to do.

## ☐ Outline

### *Ephesians: Gods Plan in Christ*

**I. Blessings in Christ**
  A. A list of blessings  *1:1–14*
  B. A prayer for growth  *1:15–23*
  C. The facts of new life  *2:1–10*

**II. Unity in Christ**
  A. Jews and Gentiles  *2:11–22*
  B. Paul's task and prayer  *3:1–21*
  C. The church's unity and diversity  *4:1–16*

**III. Living in Christ**
  A. Imitators of God  *4:17–5:20*
  B. Christian households  *5:21–6:9*
  C. The Christian's defense  *6:10–24*

# 15

□ **PRAY** for insight into God's Word

Master of the Universe, open my eyes and my ears to receive your message right now.

□ **READ** Ephesians 1:1–6

□ **MEDITATE** on God's Word

*Discovery*

**1.** In what two ways did Paul describe himself (1)? What two words did he use to describe his original readers (1)?

_____

**2.** What do you learn about God in verses 3–6?

_____

_____

**3.** Why do you suppose Paul used words like "chose" (4) and "destined" (5) to describe the Ephesians' relationship with God? For you, what does it mean to be chosen by God? What is encouraging about such a thought?

_____

_____

*Note: he chose us in him (4)—"The doctrine of election is a divine revelation, not a human speculation. It was not invented by Augustine of Hippo or Calvin of Geneva. On the contrary, it is without question a biblical doctrine, and no biblical Christian can ignore it. According to the Old Testament, God chose Israel out of the nations of the world to be his special people (Exod. 19:4–6; Deut. 7:6ff; Isa. 41:1 and 43:1). According to the New Testament he is choosing an international community to be his saints (Eph. 1:1; 1 Pet. 2:9–10). So we must not reject the notion of election as if it were a weird fantasy of men, but rather humbly accept it (even though we do not fully understand it) as a truth which God himself has revealed" (John R. W. Stott, God's New Society, [InterVarsity Press, 1979], p. 37).*

**4.** How do you define spiritual blessings? Who is their source (3, 6)? What spiritual blessings have you actually experienced this year because you believe in Jesus?

_____

_____

*Note: every spiritual blessing (3)—"From Him (Jesus Christ) comes one continuous flow of blessing, and this is to be conceived not chiefly in terms of material gifts of which we think most readily, but in terms of the spiritual blessings that transcend but include the material, for the true appreciation of the things we see is dependent on our enjoyment of the things of the Spirit" (Francis Foulkes, The Epistle of Paul to the Ephesians, Tyndale New Testament Commentaries [Eerdmans, 1956], p. 45).*

## *Reflection*

When you or I sit down to write a letter today, we usually begin with some light chitchat topics and get to our main points after a few paragraphs. Not Paul. He packed the first six verses of his letter to the Ephesians with some important truths that are integral to the rest of the Epistle. Notice how he started with:

*A bold claim (1).* Paul described himself as "an apostle" (1). He was not one of the original Twelve, but he had seen the risen Lord, and had been sent by God to preach Good News to the Gentiles. Thus his words carried great authority.

*A bold title (1).* He described his readers as "saints." In the New Testament the word is used to describe all followers of Jesus. Every Christian is called by God to live a holy life.

*A bold link (2).* As a Jewish rabbi, Paul had taught that "the Lord our God is one." As a Christian, he still believed that great truth. But he worshiped God the Son, as well as God the Father. So he linked the phrases "God" and "Father of the Lord Jesus Christ" (2).

*Bold statements (3-6).* Read through verses 3-6 again and look for the phrases with the word "us" to find some wonderful truths. And note that we can receive the benefits of these truths only when we are "in Christ" (3). Are you?

## *My Response*

## *Memory Point*

Write Ephesians 2:8-10 (Key Verse 4) on a 3 x 5 card and tape or place it in a familiar spot. Throughout the day, whenever you see the card, read the verses aloud.

## ☐ PRAY to apply God's Word

Think of the three most precious spiritual blessings you have received and open your heart in thanks to God for them . . .

# 16

☐ **PRAY for insight into God's Word**

"O loving Jesus, King of eternal glory, in the Kingdom of Thy Father, remember me, Thy poor one; and send to me now from Heaven the Holy Ghost, the Comforter, to be my true solace, with a fresh fervor, and a fuller pouring forth of the gifts of the Spirit of God. Amen" *(Thomas à Kempis).*

☐ **READ Ephesians 1:7-14**

☐ **MEDITATE on God's Word**

*Discovery*

**1.** List the benefits of being in Christ that Paul gives in these verses.

_____

_____

_____

**2.** How would you rephrase verses 7 and 8 so they could be understood by a child? By a nonbeliever?

_____

_____

_____

_____

**3.** What do you learn here about the Holy Spirit (13-14)?

_____

_____

**4.** What decision have you made to insure that verses 13-14 are true for you? How has the Holy Spirit been active in your life in the last six months?

_____

_____

## Reflection

The key to understanding Paul's letter to the Ephesians, and your own Christian life as well, is to understand what it means to be "in Christ." To Paul this was no glib phrase. Being "in Christ" should completely change a person's life and goals and entitle him to these marvelous spiritual blessings:

*In him we have redemption (7).* By Christ's death we have been set free—from sin, from fear, and from death.

*In him we have forgiveness (7).* When God forgives he doesn't keep any record of our sins. (Is that also true of you?)

*In him we have understanding (9).* God has shown us all that we need to know for the present. We know of his love in giving us freedom and forgiveness. We know, too, that he plans to unite all things in perfect harmony (10).

*In him we have a task (10).* What is this task? Reread verse 12, and pray over it.

*In him we have the Holy Spirit (13).* Those who respond to the gospel are sealed by God with his Holy Spirit. This is a guarantee of God's ownership, and also a guarantee of the good things yet to come (14).

## My Response

## Memory Point

Before each meal today, mentally or verbally recite Key Verse 4 (Eph. 2:8-10) three times.

## ☐ PRAY to apply God's Word

Ask God to give you a more intimate relationship with his "Guarantee" (13-14) to you . . .

# *17*

Lord, I confess that my hunger for your Word is not as strong as it should be or even as strong as I'd like it to be. Please let me taste the excitement of meeting you personally in what I am about to read and study . . .

☐ **READ Ephesians 1:15-23**

☐ **MEDITATE on God's Word**

### Discovery

**1.** What two things about the Ephesian church had become well known (15)?

_____

**2.** Give one-word summaries of Paul's requests for the Ephesians. Why do you suppose he prayed for these things (17–19)?

_____

_____

_____

**3.** What do these verses say about God's plan for Christ?

_____

_____

_____

**4.** Explain what Paul meant by "the hope to which he has called you" (18). What is *your* hope? How does it affect your daily actions?

_____

_____

_____

Note: the hope to which he has called you (18)—"Hope for the Christian is not to be thought of as an uncertain feeling of mingled longing and misgiving, as when we say that we hope it will be a fine day tomorrow. . . . Christian hope is a glad confidence in good things to come. It is sure, not tentative. This hope refers . . . to the certainty of life with Christ in heaven which awaits the Christian beyond death" (C. Leslie Mitton, Ephesians, New Century Bible [Marshall, Morgan and Scott, 1976], p. 68).

### Reflection

In our world, people strive desperately to be the greatest, whether in sports, business, politics, or even appearance! In these verses, however, we find that being in Christ helps us appreciate what true greatness really is. Paul tells us about:

*The greatest prayer that can be prayed.* Do you sometimes have to pray for someone about whom you know very little—someone, perhaps, from whom you have not heard for some time? Verse 15 shows us that Paul was not in regular touch with the Christians at Ephesus. What do you ask God to give someone in a case like that? The best request is for the *knowledge of Christ* (17). You can pray no greater prayer than this, for the answer to every other prayer can be found in knowing Christ better and better.

*The greatest power that can be experienced.* This earth has never seen greater power at work than the "mighty power" that raised Christ from the dead (19-20). The power of great nations, great rulers, or great weapons is nothing by comparison. Yet, all the "incomparably great power" (19) is offered us to meet our every need. Do *you* have to face a situation that needs more power than that?

*The greatest position that can be occupied.* Note carefully the position which Paul tells us has been given to Christ (20-23). He is supreme in the world, in the heavens, and in the church. He reigns, and he has ample power to reign with. So why should we fear? Why should we doubt?

### My Response

### Memory Point

Repeat Key Verse 4 (Eph. 2:8–10) aloud until you say it perfectly three times in a row. Also, think how you might use the verse in a witnessing situation.

### ☐ PRAY to apply God's Word

Using Paul's example, pray for the following people: the Christian who means the most to you, a Christian you don't like, a Christian who is in need of God's guidance now . . .

# 18

**PRAY for insight into God's Word**

"Oh loving God, be pleased, I pray Thee, but not with the good deeds that I bring before Thee. Wilt Thou consider only this, that Thou art holy and friendly, and not that I am evil. Amen" *(Martin Luther).*

□ **READ Ephesians 2:1-10** (For a change of pace, read these verses aloud.)

□ **MEDITATE on God's Word**

*Discovery*

**1.** How does Paul describe life without God (1-3)? Without God, whom do we serve—consciously or unconsciously (2)? Explain the phrase, "objects of wrath" (3).

_____

_____

**2.** What phrase does Paul use in verses 5 and 8? What does this phrase mean? Why is it so important for our understanding of salvation?

_____

_____

_____

**3.** Because of Jesus Christ, the Ephesians' lifestyle had been completely changed. What changes occurred in your life when you first accepted Christ as Savior? What is the most recent change you've made because of him?

_____

_____

_____

**4** What are "works" (9)? When are they important? When are they unimportant? What would you say to someone who said, "If you try to do good and help people, God will let you into heaven"?

_____

_____

_____

_____

### Reflection

Since Paul, in chapter one, had spelled out the incredible benefits of life in Christ, he naturally would describe life without Christ in terms of the sharpest contrast.

*Then (1-3).* Paul was a realist. He was unsentimental about human nature. He observed greed and lust in the world around him. He knew the sins of pride and hatred from his own experience, for they once led him to kill and persecute others. And he knew that, if unchecked, they would have destroyed his own spirit. So he was not exaggerating when he described the human situation in terms of death (1), disobedience (2), and wrath (3). A quick look at our modern world shows that nothing has changed.

*Now (5-7).* Despite all this, his message was full of hope and joy. He and his readers may once have been spiritually dead. But now they were alive (5) and could enjoy wonderful new life in Christ (6).

*Why?* What accounts for this transformation? What joins "then" and "now"? The answer is to be found in verses 4 and 5. Read them—and marvel at God's grace and mercy.

*How?* If God's love is *the reason* we can pass from death to life, what is *the method?* How can human beings bridge the gap between "then" and "now"; between death and life? Surely the answer must be *by great personal effort.* No! (9). Not by effort, but *by simple faith.* True, the Christian life involves "good works" (10). But we do these in grateful response to God's love. Faith means accepting God's gift with a simple "thank you."

### My Response

### Memory Point

Read Key Verse 4 (Eph. 2:8-10) in a translation other than the one you memorized (several others, if available). To you, what is the most significant truth in these verses?

### ☐ PRAY to apply God's Word

Ask God to show you one good work you could perform this week. Then ask him to help you do it with a humble spirit . . .

# 5/Ephesians 2:11–4:16
# Unity in Christ

☐ **Introduction**

One winter evening as I walked home from work, I met a very pleasant young man who started a conversation with me and invited me to join him for dinner with some friends at his house. I could tell from our conversation that the man was a member of a popular cult. I politely told him "no thanks."

Although I had given no reason for turning him down, he burst into an honest but exasperated monologue. "You know, Christians are so divided. There are so many denominations. What's so bad about the way our church tries to help people find God and tries to cause more unity?"

This young man was really searching for answers and he was frustrated. So I answered him. "Well, the only way to find God is through faith in Jesus Christ. I'm afraid that your teachers don't believe that. And if you follow them you'll be prevented from accepting Jesus as your Savior and you'll never get right with God." After a little more discussion, we split. He went to his dinner. I went home. But as I walked away I felt sad. True, there are so many groups who are successful in leading people away from God's kingdom. There are many false prophets preying on the vulnerabilities and appealing to the idealism of the young. But the young man I talked to had a point. Christians *are* divided.

Today there are thousands of Christian denominations. Worse yet, many denominations look down at and distrust others. Unfortunately, Christians are often more eager to divide than they are to stay together. Some people seem to think, "the further we divide, the holier we must be."

But the apostle Paul's command directly contradicts this reasoning. He encourages us to "keep the unity of the Spirit through the bond of peace" (4:3). In the first century the big division was between Jewish Christians and Gentile Christians. As you examine what Paul said about Christian unity in that touchy situation, try to pick out the principles that apply to our situation today. We Christians desperately need to hear them.

It is all too easy, however, to point a finger and say "Christians are too divided," and forget about the tricky questions involved. What are the limits to Christian unity? Should we accept all other groups regardless of what they do or don't believe? And during my conversation with the friendly young man, should my ideas about Christian unity have motivated me to accept a religious cult like the one he represented?

The way Paul would have answered is by pointing to Jesus. Any person or group who claims Jesus Christ as Head—that is, Jesus Christ as Lord—must be accepted (4:15-16). But there can be no Christian unity with those who do not acknowledge Jesus Christ as Lord. They are not part of the same Body.

As you complete these next five studies, ask God to teach you about unity in Christ. And more than that, ask him to give you the courage to act on what he says to you.

### □ Key Verse 5: Ephesians 4:15-16

Instead, speaking the truth in love, we will in all things grow up into him who is the Head, that is, Christ. From him the whole body, joined and held together by every supporting ligament, grows and builds itself up in love, as each part does its work.

### □ Outline

*Ephesians: God's Plan in Christ*

I.  Blessings in Christ
    A. A list of blessings  *1:1-14*
    B. A prayer for growth  *1:15-23*
    C. The facts of new life  *2:1-10*

**II. Unity in Christ**
    **A. Jews and Gentiles  *2:11-22***
    **B. Paul's task and prayer  *3:1-21***
    **C. The church's unity and diversity  *4:1-16***

III. Living in Christ
    A. Imitators of God  *4:17-5:20*
    B. Christian households  *5:21-6:9*
    C. The Christian's defense  *6:10-24*

# 19

**PRAY for insight into God's Word**
"As the deer pants for streams of water, so my soul pants for you, O God. My soul thirsts for God, for the living God" (Ps. 42:1-2a).

☐ **READ Ephesians 2:11-22**

☐ **MEDITATE on God's Word**

*Discovery*
**1.** Before Christ, what relationship did the Gentiles have with God (11-12)? What did Jesus do to repair this relationship (13, 16)? How did Jesus' work affect the relationship of Jew to Gentile?

_____

_____

_____

**2.** What was the "old way" of coming to God that Jesus abolished (15)? What is the "new way" of coming to God that he established (18)?

_____

_____

**3.** The Jews were prejudiced against the Gentiles. In the area where you live, is there a similar group of people—one whom many are prejudiced against? Are these attitudes seen in your church or fellowship? What do these verses instruct you to do about such a situation?

_____

_____

_____

**4.** Although you may not be separated from God as the Gentiles were, do you sometimes feel far away from him? Why? What could you do to get closer to God?

_____

_____

_____

### Reflection

The first disciples, like Jesus himself, were Jews. As a result, they faced a very big question. Could Gentiles become Christians without becoming Jews first? For a while, the question was in the balance and it created a considerable blockade to unity among the early Christians. But when it came, the answer was a clear Yes. Reread verse 12 to find five tragic features of our situation without Christ. But we can thank God that things have changed. Now we are:

*Reconciled to God.* By dying on the cross, Jesus broke down the barrier which sin erects between man and God (16).

*Reconciled to each other.* Jews despised Gentiles; Gentiles disliked Jews. If a Jew married a Gentile, the family had a funeral service. As far as they were concerned, he or she was dead. But Jesus broke down this barrier of hostility. His great message was "peace" (17). This same message was for those who were far away (Gentiles), and also for those who were near (Jews). In Christ's church, Jew and Gentile were to be:
—fellow citizens (19)
—fellow members of God's household (19)
—one holy temple with a common foundation (20–21)
—indwelt by the Spirit of the one God (22).

Today, people are polarized in a variety of ways: rich and poor, black and white, young and old, Republican and Democrat, Protestant and Catholic. We need to boldly demonstrate Christ's love in these situations, relying on the Holy Spirit's power to prevent them from disrupting our unity in Christ.

### My Response

### Memory Point

Write Key Verse 5 (Eph. 4:15–16) on a 3 x 5 card and place or tape it in a familiar spot. Repeat it at least ten times today.

### ☐ PRAY to apply God's Word

Talk to God about your relationship with people you have trouble accepting . . .

# 20

☐ **PRAY for insight into God's Word**

Close your eyes and quiet yourself before God. Each time you exhale think of a concern or worry you wish to give God. Each time you inhale ask the Holy Spirit to fill you and be with you during your study today.

☐ **READ Ephesians 3:1–13**

☐ **MEDITATE on God's Word**

*Discovery*

**1.** What does Paul say his calling was (1–7, 8–10)? Before he embarked on this mission, what was he (Saul) doing (see Acts 9:1–2)? Why is it significant that Paul is now preaching to the Gentiles?

_____

_____

_____

**2.** Give a dictionary definition of the word "mystery." What is the mystery to which Paul refers (3, 4, 9)? What does the term mystery indicate about Paul's Good News?

_____

_____

*Note: the mystery (3)—"This is the divinely revealed truth which relates to the inclusion of the Gentiles in a church wherever all barriers of race are broken down" (Ralph P. Martin, The New Bible Commentary: Revised, Ephesians [Eerdmans, 1970], p. 1113).*

**3.** Paul shows special concern for evangelizing the Gentiles. What group or kind of person are you especially eager to share the gospel with? Why? How could you put this eagerness into action in the next week or month? If you're not eager to share the Good News with anybody, what should you do?

_____

_____

_____

**4.** Paul freely uses terms like "mystery" and "unsearchable" when talking about the gospel. Do you think many modern Christians are uncomfortable with mysteries and have tried to "nail everything down"? If so, why? How does this tendency affect the unity among Christians?

_____

_____

_____

### Reflection

"The mystery" (4, 9) of which Paul speaks refers to what had previously been a kind of secret—that the Gentiles as well as the Jews are included in the gospel (6) and share "the unsearchable riches of Christ" (8). Notice how this wonderful gospel is unfolded to man. It began in the "*wisdom* of God" (10), and was part of his "eternal purpose" (11) for the world. It became effective through *the work* of Christ upon the Cross (11), and finally it is being made known to the world through the *witness* of the church (10). Notice the modesty with which Paul, the great leader of the church, accepted the privilege of this work (8).

Throughout the life of Paul we can detect a growing humility as he came to know Christ better. Is that also true in your life? Quite early in his ministry Paul tells us that he is "the least of the apostles" and does "not even deserve to be called an apostle" (1 Cor. 15:9). Here, in midcareer, he calls himself "less than the least of all God's people" (8). (Notice his disregard for grammar. How can anyone be "less than the least"?) At the end of his life (1 Tim. 1:15) he sees himself as the worst of sinners. How true is the hymn which says, "They who fain would serve Thee best are conscious most of wrong within"!

### My Response

### Memory Point

Face yourself in a mirror and repeat Key Verse 5 (Eph. 4:15-16) three times looking at your eyes as you speak.

### ☐ PRAY to apply God's Word

Think of a non-Christian person or group with whom you have a good relationship. Ask God for an opportunity to share the gospel with that person or group this month . . .

# 21

□ **PRAY for insight into God's Word**

"Open my eyes to see wonderful things in Your Word" (Ps. 119:18 TLB).

□ **READ Ephesians 3:14-21**

□ **MEDITATE on God's Word**

*Discovery*

**1.** List the elements of Paul's prayer for the Ephesians (14-19). Explain what each element means and how it is accomplished in a person's life.

_____

_____

_____

_____

*Note: the inner man (16 RSV)—"The inner man was a phrase which the Greeks knew and used. By the inner man the Greeks understood three things. (a) There was a man's reason. [Paul] wanted them to be better able to discern between that which was right and that which was wrong . . . (b) There was conscience . . . It was the prayer of Paul that Jesus should keep our consciences tender and on the alert. (c) There was the will. It is the essential weakness of life that . . . we know what is right, but our will is not strong enough to back our knowledge" (William Barclay, The Letter to the Galatians and the Ephesians, The Daily Study Bible Series [The Westminster Press, 1956], pp. 153-154).*

*Note: the power at work within us (16)—"The ability of God to work beyond our prayers, thoughts and dreams is by the power at work within us, within us individually (Christ dwelling in our hearts by faith) and within us as a people (who are the dwelling place of God by his Spirit). It is the power of the resurrection, the power which raised Christ from the dead, enthroned him in the heavenlies, and then raised and enthroned us there with him. That is the power at work within the Christian and the church" (John R. W. Stott, God's New Society, The Bible Speaks Today [Inter-Varsity Press, 1979], p. 140).*

**2.** What does Paul's posture during prayer (14) show about his attitude toward God? What posture do you take when praying? Why? Is it possible to be too casual about our prayer habits? How? What are the most important ingredients in a healthy prayer life?

_____

_____

_____

**3.** In what specific, practical ways have you experienced the love of Christ (19)? In what sense do these experiences surpass knowledge? What actions has Christ's love motivated you to attempt in the last year?

_____

_____

_____

_____

### Reflection

In these verses Paul again shifts gears and shares the substance of his frequent prayers for his readers. In so doing, he tactfully points out how they can grow in the Christian life.

*Be humble.* Paul often speaks about the free access we have to God. We are to come to God with boldness and confidence because Jesus has opened the way (12). We come as children to our Father. But we are to come with great respect. Paul sets an example. He comes before God in humility—on his knees (14).

*Be strong.* As he kneels, he prays. His prayer is that the Christians in his care may be inwardly strong. What is our source of strength (16)?

*Be rooted.* What is the truest test of discipleship? Jesus gave the answer. "All men will know that you are my disciples if you love one another" (John 13:35). Paul's prayer is that the Ephesians may have roots which go deep into the soil of love.

*Be wise.* Because of Jesus, we know the vast dimensions of God's love (18). But the true greatness of that love is more than we can grasp; it "surpasses knowledge" (19). God's love is not something just to be "known" in some academic way. It is to be experienced and enjoyed—that's what lies behind Paul's prayer.

*Be united.* These great blessings are for each Christian. But they cannot be developed in isolation. "To him be glory *in the church*" (21). We must grow *together*.

### My Response




### Memory Point

Write Key Verse 5 (Eph. 4:15-16) on a piece of paper and put it in your wallet or purse. Whenever you see it mentally or verbally recite it and think of a way to put the verse into action in that immediate situation.

### ☐ PRAY to apply God's Word

If possible, kneel as you pray today. Start with confession, move to thanksgiving and finish by praying for the Christians you will see in the next week . . .

# 22

☐ **PRAY for insight into God's Word**
Lord God, I thank you for the ability to think clearly. Help me to carefully examine this passage and uncover your truth.

☐ **READ Ephesians 4:1–6**

☐ **MEDITATE on God's Word**

### Discovery

**1.** List the qualities of a worthy life (2–3) and give a practical example of each that you have seen recently.

_____

_____

**2.** What does Paul seem to be emphasizing in verses 4–6? Why do you suppose this was so important to him?

_____

_____

**3.** Do verses 3–6 accurately describe the attitude found among Christian groups you know? Why or why not? What would you say to a person who said, "Christians squabble so much among themselves that I don't want to get involved in a church"? What could you do to promote unity in your church this year?

_____

_____

_____

**4.** Are there limits to Christian unity? Under what circumstances, if any, is division necessary? When is it wrong? What would you advise a Christian who asked, "Should I continue as a member of my church denomination since they seem to be veering from what I believe the Bible teaches on certain crucial points?"

_____

_____

_____

_____

### Reflection

"How good and pleasant it is when brothers live together in unity!" These words from Psalm 133:1 could sum up the message of today's verses. Harmony, not discord, is to govern relations between Christians, even though their temperaments or interests may be completely different. Paul deals here with two ways in which we can strengthen this unity.

*A proud spirit must be ruled out* (1-2). You know, divisions between Christians are largely caused by proud people who love the sound of their own voices. If you have two Christians, perhaps of different denominations, living in the spirit of verses 1 and 2, there is likely to be little friction between them. It's much harder to fall out with someone you love!

*A separatist spirit must be ruled out* (3-6). Another cause of strife is that some people love to have a point of view to campaign for. They stick up for their own particular group of Christians against other groups of Christians. They pick on minor differences and make them seem vitally important; they do not realize the harm they are doing to the work of Christ. All who hold to the "one faith" and worship the "one Lord" must realize that they belong to "one body," and act accordingly.

### My Response

### Memory Point

Review Key Verse 4 (Eph. 2:8-10) by saying it aloud from memory and by reflecting on its significance to you. Then repeat Key Verse 5 (Eph. 4:15-16) until you say it without making a mistake.

### ☐ PRAY to apply God's Word

Bring before God a situation in your church or group where unity is lacking . . .

# 23

□ **PRAY for insight into God's Word**
"O Thou Lord of life, send my roots rain" *(Gerard Manley Hopkins).*

□ **READ Ephesians 4:7–16**

□ **MEDITATE on God's Word**

*Discovery*
**1.** To whom are spiritual gifts given (7)? List the gifts Paul mentions (11). Does this list of "gifts" appear to be all-inclusive?

_____

_____

**2.** What are some potential problems for a church lacking unity (14)?

_____

_____

**3.** How does Paul say growth occurs in a church (16)? Is this the prevailing view-point in your church? What are the dangers of leaving all the church work to the "professionals"?

_____

_____

_____

**4.** What does it mean to "speak the truth in love" (15)? Is this sort of speech always positive and friendly? Why? Give examples you have seen or experienced. In what situation do you need to speak the truth in love this week?

_____

_____

_____

_____

## Reflection

In our last four studies, we've learned that Christian unity is vitally important. But how are we fallible, sin-prone human beings ever supposed to develop into the strong and healthy body God wants us to become? Paul says the solution comes through exercising our spiritual gifts and he addresses himself to three aspects of this topic.

*The giver.* Using a quotation from Psalm 68, Paul points out that Jesus is uniquely placed to give gifts to us. He *descended* to earth; he shared our life, so he knows our needs. Then he *ascended* to heaven, which is filled with his glory.

*The gifts.* He gave gifts to his church (11). There are other lists in the New Testament—none is identical (1 Cor. 12:4-11; Rom. 12:3-8). We should beware of saying, "There are *x* number of gifts and they are these." Christ knows just what is needed in any situation.

*The outcome.* God's gifts are given to individuals. But they are intended to build up the whole church (12). In particular, apostles, prophets, evangelists, pastors and teachers should encourage unity, knowledge of Jesus, and maturity among Christians (13). In this way two qualities will be assured:

—*Stability.* Sound example and teaching are the best defense against crafty and deceitful schemes (14).

—*Growth.* They also ensure that the Christian community will grow as a healthy body, with Christ as the head.

## My Response

## Memory Point

Review Key Verses 1, 2, and 3. What does Key Verse 5 (Eph. 4:15-17) teach you about Christian unity?

## ☐ PRAY to apply God's Word

If you haven't yet discovered it, ask God to show you what your spiritual gift is. If you know what it is, ask him for an opportunity to strengthen the Body of Christ with it this month . . .

# 6/Ephesians 4:17–6:24
# Living in Christ

□ **Introduction**

Every so often I see a particular bumper sticker which irritates me. It has a two-word message, usually in big block letters, that simply says "QUESTION AUTHORITY." I normally spot this bumper sticker on the back of a worn-out Volvo or a beat-up Volkswagen.

In any case, what irritates me about the bumper sticker is its assumption that no authority is legitimate—whether it be government, the church, employers, parents or any other—unless the owner of the bumper sticker happens to think so.

"QUESTION AUTHORITY" seems to be a pious euphemism for saying, "No one, not even God, has the authority to tell me how to live. I tell myself how to live."

But as Christians, those who have accepted Jesus Christ as Savior and Lord, we are under an Authority which we dare never question. When God tells us how we ought to live, our reflex must be to obey.

In the next seven studies God's Word will tell you how to live. Paul is the one God used to express these guidelines for living. And if on some points you are tempted to think, "Ah, that's just Paul's opinion, not God's," remember that Paul was "an apostle of Christ Jesus by the will of God" and his letter is now part of Holy Scripture.

Sometimes Paul peppers us with lists of staccato commands: don't steal, no foul talk, don't get drunk, forgive others. Other times he elaborates on subjects which are especially important, like relationships between husbands and wives, parents and children, masters and slaves. But Paul ends his letter to the Ephesians on a refreshingly practical note. As you study it you probably won't have trouble answering the question, "What does this mean?" Rather, a much more challenging question will be, "How can I put this into action?"

One word of caution, though. The secret to successful living in Christ is not merely the keeping of rules. The guidelines Paul spells out for us are intended to help us "put on the new self, created to be like God" (4:24). The secret is in everything we do to "be imitators of God" (5:1). And the best way for us to do this is to focus on Jesus. How would Jesus act? What would he do or say? How did Jesus relate to others and his Father?

Whenever we take our eyes off of Jesus and concentrate only on rules, we leave ourselves wide open to the frustrations of a joyless Christian life at best and hypocritical legalism at worst.

As you begin these remaining studies in Ephesians, ask God for a balanced understanding of his commands for living in Christ. And, too, ask the Holy Spirit for a new appreciation for what it means to "be made new in the attitude of your minds" (4:23).

## ☐ Key Verse 6: Ephesians 5:8-10

For you were once darkness, but now you are light in the Lord. Live as children of light (for the fruit of the light consists in all goodness, righteousness and truth) and find out what pleases the Lord.

## ☐ Outline

### *Ephesians: God's Plan in Christ*

I. Blessings in Christ
   A. A list of blessings  *1:1-14*
   B. A prayer for growth  *1:15-23*
   C. The facts of new life  *2:1-10*

II. Unity in Christ
   A. Jews and Gentiles  *2:11-22*
   B. Paul's task and prayer  *3:1-21*
   C. The church's unity and diversity  *4:1-16*

III. **Living in Christ**
   A. **Imitators of God**  *4:17-5:20*
   B. **Christian households**  *5:21-6:9*
   C. **The Christian's defense**  *6:10-24*

**24**

☐ **PRAY for insight into God's Word**
"Blessed Lord, who hast caused all holy Scriptures to be written for our learning, grant that we may in such wise hear them, read, mark, learn, and inwardly digest them, that by patience, and comfort of Thy holy Word, we may embrace, and even hold fast the blessed hope of everlasting life, which Thou hast given us in our Saviour Jesus Christ. Amen" *(The Book of Common Prayer).*

☐ **READ Ephesians 4:17–24**

☐ **MEDITATE on God's Word**

*Discovery*
**1.** How did Paul describe the Gentile unbelievers in Ephesus (17–19)? What was the root of all these characteristics (18b)?

_____

_____

**2.** In what ways were the Ephesian Christians to be different from these Gentile unbelievers? What instructions did Paul give to counteract the evil influences (22–24)?

_____

_____

_____

**3.** What attitudes or actions seem to alienate you from God? What causes you to become hard or callous toward God? How do you overcome these problems?

_____

_____

_____

**4.** Why is it important to "put on" after you have "put off"? What activities and thoughts have you laid aside because of your relationship with Christ? What quality are you *currently* trying to put on? How could you work on it this week?

_____

_____

_____

_____

### Reflection

At this point in the letter, Paul turned his attention to the nitty-gritty details about how the Ephesians should and should not live.

*Darkness in Ephesus.* The Christian life involves positive qualities—love, faith, hope, peace, forgiveness, patience. But it includes some negative features too. There are certain attitudes that must be avoided, and some things we must not do. At this point Paul concentrated on these negative aspects—with good reason. He knew Ephesus well. It was an important port, an international meeting place. And as the center for the worship of Diana, it was noted for its immorality.

*Hope from Ephesus.* Paul painted a very dark picture of life in Ephesus (18–19). Was he exaggerating? No! Historians confirm Paul's view. Strangely, this gives great hope. The world in which the Christian gospel took root was not marked by light and love. It was a dark, cruel, hopeless world. If our own world sometimes seems like this, take heart! The Good News can still spread and defeat the forces of darkness.

*Living in Ephesus.* To those surrounded by such darkness, Paul makes two practical points, just as relevant to us now as to the first readers in Ephesus:
—*Put off your old self (22).* Most of his readers had experienced the pagan lifestyle of Ephesus. Despite its darkness, some of them continued to find it attractive. Don't play with fire, commanded Paul.
—*Put on the new self.* What are the characteristics which mark this nature (24)?

### My Response

### Memory Point

Write out Key Verse 6 (Eph. 5:8–10) on a 3 x 5 card and tape or place it in a familiar spot. Throughout the day, whenever you see it, read the verses aloud and think about what they mean.

### ☐ PRAY to apply God's Word

Pray about one aspect of your old nature you need to put off. Ask the Holy Spirit to help you put on the part of the new nature you need the most . . .

**25**

☐ **PRAY for insight into God's Word**
Lift your hands up, open your eyes and praise God out loud for three things as you begin this study.

☐ **READ Ephesians 4:25-32**

☐ **MEDITATE on God's Word**

*Discovery*
**1.** Find the direct commands in this passage and rephrase them in a way that highlights their meaning to you.

_____

_____

_____

**2.** What are the reasons Paul gives for following these commands (4:25b, 27, 28b, 32b)? How do the reasons relate to the commands?

_____

_____

**3.** Which one of these specific commands is most difficult for you to obey? Why? What helps you obey this command? What tempts you to disobey it?

_____

_____

_____

_____

**4.** How does a person grieve the Holy Spirit (30)? What habits, activities or attitudes of yours may be grieving the Holy Spirit now? What can you do about them?

_____

_____

_____

_____

### Reflection

In these verses we find two blueprints for living. The Devil has one; so does God. If we belong to Christ and want to build real Christian character, we must see that we follow *God's* plans.

*Satan's blueprint.* We should know what is in this blueprint, not in order to follow it, but in order to avoid it. Look for each of these items in today's verses, and notice what we are to do about each one.
—*Sin of the heart:* uncontrolled anger, a bitter spirit.
—*Sin of the hands:* stealing.
—*Sin of the lips:* lying, bad language, slanderous talk.

We must make a complete break with all these things; we must abandon Satan's blueprint utterly, and give him no foothold whatsoever (27).

*God's blueprint.* As Christians, we have a *new plan* to follow in building our *new life.* For every part of Satan's plan, God has something better. Here are the things to look for, and you can compare them with the first list.
—*For the heart:* self-control, compassion.
—*For the hands:* hard work and generosity.
—*For the lips:* love of truth, gracious speech, words of forgiveness.

Verse 32 suggests that if we faithfully follow this pattern we shall become like Christ, for Christ himself fulfilled it perfectly in every point. He deserves our praise for that!

### My Response

### Memory Point

Repeat Key Verse 6 (Eph. 5:8–10) until you can say it three times in a row without looking and without mistakes. Repeat this exercise just before you go to bed tonight. (Leave your 3 x 5 card on your pillow or bedside table so you'll remember!)

### ☐ PRAY to apply God's Word

Choose the command from this passage which is most difficult for you to obey and talk to God about it now . . .

# 26

☐ **PRAY for insight into God's Word**

"Expound to me the way of Your statues, Yahweh, and I will always respect them. Explain to me how to respect Your law and how to observe it wholeheartedly. Guide me in the path of Your commandments, since my delight is there. Turn my heart to Your decrees and away from getting money. Avert my eyes from lingering on inanities, and give me life by your Word" (Ps. 119:33-37, JB).

☐ **READ Ephesians 5:1-14**

☐ **MEDITATE on God's Word**

*Dis overy*

**1.** What image does Paul use in 5:2? Further describe this image. What does he communicate about love by using the word "fragrant"?

_____

_____

**2.** Contrast what Paul says about the deeds of light and of darkness (8-14).

_____

_____

_____

**3.** In this passage Paul gives us several specific commands. List the three that are the most relevant to you and give examples of how you could better obey each one.

_____

_____

_____

**4.** Can God's forgiveness extend to the person in verse 5? How would you counsel a Christian who had sinned in one of these areas?

_____

_____

_____

### Reflection

Paul begins chapter 5 with an almost impossible standard of living: "Be imitators of God." Jesus was able to do this perfectly (2) and we must follow his example. But the apostle knew you and I would need more help than that so he gets very specific in verses 3–14.

*Unsuitable activities.* Paul is blunt. Some things are wrong—so wrong that we should not even talk about them, let alone do them. Doubtful jokes are out; thanksgiving is in (3-4)! Impurity has no place in the kingdom of God, nor has covetousness. We must not hanker after things which belong to other people.

*Unsuitable relationships.* Paul is writing to adult converts, those who have first-hand experience of pagan immorality. To avoid the downward pull of their old lifestyle drastic measures are needed. So Paul says, don't form close relationships with those who live the way you used to (7).

*Suitable alternatives.* In the darkness we need light; the Ephesian Christians lived in a dark world. They, and we, are to take positive action by:
—living as children of light (8), and that will mean showing the fruit of light as described in verse 9.
—trying to learn what is pleasing to the Lord (10).
—exposing the works of darkness (11).

Paul concludes his meditation on light by quoting an early Christian hymn (14). It combines a strong command—wake up!—with a wonderful promise, *Christ will shine on you.* What a phrase to meditate on!

### My Response

### Memory Point

As you mentally review Key Verse 6 (Eph. 5:8-10), meditate on the light of Christ's presence illuminating your life this day.

### ☐ PRAY to apply God's Word

Evaluate your speech in the light of today's Bible passage. Ask God to forgive you for any ways you've misused it recently. Then ask him for an opportunity to use your words for his glory today . . .

# 27

☐ **PRAY for insight into God's Word**
Dear Jesus, I want to hear your voice. Help me to listen carefully as I complete this study and throughout this day.

☐ **READ Ephesians 5:15-20**

☐ **MEDITATE on God's Word**

*Discovery*
**1.** Why must we be careful (15)? Why should the evil around us motivate us to "make the most of every opportunity" (16)?

_____

_____

_____

**2.** How does Paul explain "being filled with the Spirit" (18b-20)? Do all these things seem *practical* to you? Why or why not?

_____

_____

_____

**3.** Paul mentions that we should "understand what the Lord's will is" (17). In what ways do you find God's will for you? Give specific examples from your life. How could finding God's will in the past help you find God's will in the future?

_____

_____

_____

_____

**4.** Verses 19-20 describe a joyous picture of Christian life. When is your Christian life most joyful? Why? How could you live a more joyful Christian life?

_____

_____

_____

### Reflection

As usual, towards the end of his letter Paul gets more and more practical as he turns his attention to Christian living.

*Watch your step.* Imagine that you are walking by flashlight on a dark night. You will step carefully. This is precisely our situation. In a dark world, we have the light of Christ (14), but we must walk with care (15). What else gives us light (see Ps. 119:105)?

*Watch the clock.* We Christians are to be alert and not lazy. Life is a gift from God, and we are stewards of our time, our energy, and our gifts. We should use them wisely, "making the most of the time" (16, RSV).

*Watch the Lord.* Avoid foolishness, says the apostle. Instead, understand what the Lord wants from you (17).

These statements are important, but general. They will involve different things for each of us, depending on our gifts, our situation, and our personality. But the next sentences are very specific.

—*Don't get drunk.* Instead, be filled with the Spirit and praise God (18–19).

—*Give thanks*—not only when we feel like it, but *always* and in the name of our Lord Jesus Christ.

### My Response

### Memory Point

Use your lunch time today to meditate on Key Verse 6 (Eph. 5:8–10); talk with God about how you could please him more.

### ☐ PRAY to apply God's Word

Ask God to help you genuinely feel and want to express the joy of knowing him this month . . .

# 28

☐ **PRAY for insight into God's Word**
Jesus, help me to know that you are real and that you are with me as I look into your Word now . . .

☐ **READ Ephesians 5:21-33**

☐ **MEDITATE on God's Word**

*Discovery*
**1.** How does verse 21 relate to Paul's instructions concerning marriage? How does it apply to your relationships with the fellow-believers with whom you have regular contact—your family, friends, or possibly coworkers?

_____

_____

**2.** From this passage, what is the wife's responsibility? What is the husband's responsibility? For whom do you think this obedience will be more costly?

_____

_____

_____

**3.** In your own words, explain what marriage teaches us about the relationship between Christ and the church.

_____

_____

_____

**4.** Do you think this passage sets up one role for husbands and wives? Is there room for variation? Why or why not?

_____

_____

_____

## Reflection

So often Paul slips almost unconsciously from the practical to the spiritual. Just as he is speaking of the ideal relationship between husband and wife, he sees the perfect illustration of what should exist between Christ and his church. Jesus Christ expects three things:

*Authority over his church (23-24).* Just as the ultimate responsibility and decision in any family matter must belong to the husband, so Christ asks us for our submission to his will.

*Sanctity in his church (26-27).* The husband's sacrificing love merits the whole of his wife's love and loyalty, which he should never share with others. Christ also wants us to be entirely his, not tarnished in any way by sin.

*Communion with his church (28-32).* The happiest marriages are those in which husband and wife share intimacy and interpersonal communion on every level. That is the sort of oneness that Christ wants for his church, as he prayed in the Garden of Gethsemane (John 17:22-23).

Notice finally what is to be the basis for this relationship. As between a husband and his wife, so also between Christ and his church, it is to be one of self-sacrificing love (25, 29)—his love for us, received and reflected back to himself.

## My Response

## Memory Point

Think of a familiar tune or make up one that fits all or a part of Key Verse 6 (Eph. 5:8-10). Sing or hum it as much as you can today, meditating on the words.

## ☐ PRAY to apply God's Word

Pray for your marriage or for the marriage of someone you care about . . .

# 29

□ **PRAY for insight into God's Word**

"Your hands made me and formed me; give me understanding to learn your commands" (Ps. 119:73).

□ **READ Ephesians 6:1–9**

□ **MEDITATE on God's Word**

*Discovery*

**1.** Review Paul's instructions about the family (1–4). Are there times when some of these instructions should *not* be obeyed? When? Why do the family and family relationships seem to be so important to Paul?

_____

_____

_____

**2.** For whom does Paul encourage slaves to work (5b)? How does this apply to you and the work you do each day? In what situations is it most difficult to put these verses into practice? What can you do about it?

_____

_____

_____

_____

**3.** What principles from verses 5–9 could you put into practice at your work or school? In the light of verse 7, how would you rate the quality of your service? In what areas or relationships could your attitude be improved?

_____

_____

_____

**4.** What goals have you set for your life? Given your unique talents and abilities, are there other goals you could pursue that would be more pleasing to God? If so, what are they and how might you go about reaching them?

_____

_____

_____

## Reflection

A major category under the topic of Christian living is relationships. Paul tackles several of these in our passage today.

*Children and parents.* The teaching is straightforward. Children are to obey their parents. To support this point, Paul quotes the fifth commandment (Exod. 20:12). But parents have responsibilities too. They are to provide discipline, instruction, and understanding. Provoking is not allowed (4)!

*Slaves and masters.* Slaves? Surely Paul should be telling Christians to set their slaves free! A good point, but there were more than fifty million slaves in the Roman Empire. To alter the entire basis of social, economic, and domestic life would have been beyond the influence of Christians. It would have created a new set of problems—homelessness, starvation, looting and possibly the collapse of order in society. So instead, he told them to treat them with dignity, as brothers. Later, the full implications of New Testament teaching gradually bore fruit.

## My Response

## Memory Point

Review Key Verses 4, 5, and 6 (Eph. 2:8-10; 4:15-16; 5:8-10). Can you still recite all three without having to look at them?

## ☐ PRAY to apply God's Word

Pray for one parent-child relationship you know of that is currently experiencing trouble. Also, if they are still living, pray for your parents today . . .

# 30

☐ **PRAY for insight into God's Word**
Lord Jesus, make this time something other than a routine Bible study. Let your Holy Spirit shake me up, challenge me, and inspire me to be one of your whole-hearted servants.

☐ **READ Ephesians 6:10-24**

☐ **MEDITATE on God's Word**

*Discovery*
**1.** List and describe the various parts of the armor of God (14–17). In what practical ways could you put on each piece of the armor?

_____

_____

_____

_____

_____

**2.** Why does Paul say the armor of God is important? From what does it protect us (11–13, 16)? What other "weapon" does Paul remind us about (18)?

_____

_____

_____

**3.** When have you been clearly aware that the spiritual warfare (12) which Paul describes is still raging today? What did you do? How could you help others who are experiencing similar circumstances?

_____

_____

_____

**4** List the three main lessons you have learned from the book of Ephesians.

_____

_____

_____

## Reflection

It's war! Every Christian is on frontline service against Satan. No one can get out of it by being too young, too old, too busy, or just plain lazy.

*Know our enemy.* We may think that our problems are just people and things. No way! Behind them lurk unseen forces determined to destroy us (12). They are commanded by Satan himself (11). We must never underestimate these powers. But at the same time, we shouldn't be afraid of them. We must fight them until they flee from us.

*Know our armor.* We must "be strong *in the Lord*" (10). To help us, God offers six pieces of armor. Two of them show that we are on the Lord's side: *the belt of truth* and *the breastplate of righteousness.* The Christian soldier must stand for the truth and do what is right, whatever the cost. Another two protect us against attack: *the shield of faith* and *the helmet of salvation,* which will deal with all the temptations and doubts Satan can hurl at us. Two more are to carry the war against the enemy: *the shoes of the Gospel* and *the sword of God's Word* will help us win victories that will cause joy for all eternity!

Today, there are many popular movies and books that treat the Devil and evil as "just another thrill," something to entertain us. But Christians should have no part in that foolish mistake. Followers of Jesus, Paul reminds us, are involved in a battle more serious than most people realize. It's important to be protected. So we must start putting on the armor of God today!

## My Response

## Memory Point

What new lesson have you learned from Key Verse 6 (Eph. 5:8-10)? What did it teach you that you didn't know two weeks ago?

## ☐ PRAY to apply God's Word

Thank God for winning the war for all eternity on Calvary . . .

# 7/Philippians 1:1–2:30
# Imitating Christ

## ☐ Introduction

Before you begin to study Philippians, go back and read the overview on page 10, which will give you a broad perspective for your daily study.

Corruption, decline, and decay are words which characterize the Christian church toward the end of the Middle Ages. It is probably fair to say that spiritually, the church reached its lowest point ever in the fourteenth and fifteenth centuries.

Christendom was being battered by heresies and weakened by internal conflict. Missionary zeal had drastically withered. There was a shortage of theological strength and, worst of all, there was a lack of spiritual leadership. The clergy were corrupt, immoral, ignorant, and hypocritical. As one historian has noted, "Corruption is one thing, official sanction of corruption is quite another. The heart of the rotten condition of the . . . church lay in papal protection and promotion of abuses."

During this time, around 1420, a man named Thomas Haemerken wrote a book. In it he demonstrated from the Scriptures that the way to truly please God—in contrast to what the official church was demonstrating—was to radically follow the example of Jesus Christ. His message had the ring of truth that men and women were longing to hear and the book became immensely popular. Since then it has become one of the most influential and widely read books in the world. The author, better known as Thomas à Kempis, titled his book *The Imitation of Christ*. By simply calling his contemporaries to imitate the life and example of Christ, he made a profound impact on the church and prepared the way for the Reformation which was soon to follow.

Actually, the message that Thomas à Kempis penned was not new. Fourteen hundred years earlier the apostle Paul had written the same thing in a letter to a group of Christians in Philippi, as you will see in your next few readings.

Paul was eminently qualified to preach such a message because, more than anything else, his life was devoted to imitating Jesus Christ. In the first two chapters of Philippians we see that Paul imitated Jesus by fearlessly preaching the gospel (1:18) and by suffering for doing so (1:12–14). Paul's opening prayer for his readers (1:3–11) is centered around his concern that they be more and more able to imitate Christ. So intense was Paul's desire to imitate Christ himself that he could say, "For to me, to live is Christ . . ." (1:21).

This theme reaches its climax in chapter two when the apostle states, "Your attitude should be the same as that of Christ Jesus . . ." and he continues with one of the most powerful descriptions of Jesus in the entire Bible (2:5–11).

As you work through the next studies, challenge yourself by asking and answering this question, "How could I more fully imitate Christ in every area of my life?" How would your behavior change if you were to radically copy the example of Jesus in your family life? Would any aspect of your lifestyle change if you made imitating Christ the focus of your day?

The apostle Paul committed himself to following the example of Jesus Christ and teaching others to do the same. As a result, God used him to accomplish the monumental task of establishing the church among the Gentiles in the first century.

This week you will have the same opportunity to get serious about imitating Jesus Christ. Ask God to help you eagerly seize this opportunity. If you do, you can expect God to deepen your fellowship with himself and begin using you to accomplish great things in the situations where he has placed you.

## ☐ Key Verse 7: Philippians 2:5–8

Your attitude should be the same as that of Christ Jesus: Who, being in very nature God, did not consider equality with God something to be grasped, but made himself nothing, taking the very nature of a servant, being made in human likeness. And being found in appearance as a man, he humbled himself and became obedient to death—even death on a cross!

## ☐ Outline

*Philippians: Paths to Joy*

I. **Imitating Christ**
   A. **Thanksgiving and prayer** *1:1–11*
   B. **Paul's example** *1:12–30*
   C. **The humility of Christ** *2:1–18*
   D. **Timothy and Epaphroditus** *2:19–30*

II. Living for the Lord
   A. New priorities *3:1–11*
   B. Pressing on *3:12–21*
   C. Rejoicing *4:1–13*
   D. Acknowledging a gift *4:14–23*

# 31

☐ **PRAY for insight into God's Word**
Dear heavenly Father, let your Holy Spirit surround me in this room right now so I may meet you in your Word today.

☐ **READ Philippians 1:1-11**

☐ **MEDITATE on God's Word**

*Discovery*
**1.** Why was Paul so thankful for the Philippian Christians (5, 7-8)?

_____

_____

**2.** Is verse 6 an encouragement to you? Why? What insight does this verse give you into God's sovereignty?

_____

_____

*Note: he who began a good work in you will bring it to completion (6)—"the thought here stresses not only the sovereign initiative of God in salvation (cf. the wording of Acts 16:14, describing the first Philippian convert) but also the sovereign faithfulness of God in Christ" (R. P. Martin, The Epistle of Paul to the Philippians, The Tyndale New Testament Commentaries [Eerdmans, 1959], p. 62).*

**3.** What seems to be the focus of Paul's prayer request for his readers (9a)? How do the other parts of his prayer relate to that main request (9b-11)?

_____

_____

**4.** For what Christian or group of Christians do you have a special love? Why? What is your prayer for that person or group? Are there ways you could help answer your own prayer this month?

_____

_____

_____

_____

## Reflection

When Paul began writing this letter to the Philippians, it seems he chose to use his standard opening formula—introduction plus greeting—so we shouldn't expect to gain much from it, right? Wrong! Look closely at the many truths the apostle wove into these opening verses.

*The introduction (1-2).* Think about the "pairs" which are referred to: Paul and Timothy—two very different men, both Christ's servants; "in Christ Jesus" and "at Philippi"—Christians have a close relationship with Christ, but they still have clear responsibility in this world; "bishops and deacons"—church leaders with different tasks; "grace and peace"—the twin benefits God gives his people; "God our Father and the Lord Jesus Christ"—the sources of all good for the believer.

*The greeting (3-11).* Here we see how deeply Paul felt for the Christians and how much he cared for them. There are three key words:

—Prayer (4, 9). Rome was a long way from Philippi, but Paul didn't forget the Philippians. He regularly remembered them and prayed for them with thankfulness. Do we always remember to pray for friends who are far away?

—Share (7). The Philippians shared in Paul's ministry; they sent him practical help (see 4:14-16) and they were also fighting in the same great cause of "the gospel" (5, 7).

—Care (7-8). "I long for all of you"; Paul was not just a professional preacher or evangelist, moving on from one group to another. He was a good shepherd, as Christ had been (John 10), and cared for them "with the affection of Christ Jesus" (8).

## My Response

## Memory Point

Write out Key Verse 7 (Phil. 2:5-8) on a 3x5 card and tape or place it in a familiar spot. Throughout the day, whenever you see it, repeat the verse aloud.

## □ PRAY to apply God's Word

Pray for the Christians with whom you will most closely associate this week using the ideas in verses 9-11 . . .

# 32

☐ **PRAY for insight into God's Word**
Begin this time today with a few minutes of self-examination and confession, kneeling if you are able.

☐ **READ Philippians 1:12–18**

☐ **MEDITATE on God's Word**

*Discovery*
**1.** In what situation does Paul find himself (13–14)? What had caused his predicament (13)?

_____

_____

**2.** What are the results of Paul's situation (12–17)? How does he react (18)?

_____

_____

**3.** What two kinds of preachers does Paul distinguish between (15–17)? Can you jot down one modern example of each? Is your attitude the same as Paul's (18) to *both* of your contemporary examples? Why or why not?

_____

_____

_____

**4.** What is the most difficult situation you've been in during the last year? How could you have used it to advance the gospel?

_____

_____

_____

_____

### Reflection

Proclaiming Christ (18) was Paul's highest joy in life. In fact, he viewed everything in terms of how it served to advance the gospel, as we see in today's reading.

*Christ proclaimed in any situation (12-14).* Sometimes we are tempted to think that evangelism (telling others what Jesus means to us) is a subject that we must study and can perform only in special circumstances (crusades, publicity blitzes, passing out tracts). But Paul's experience shows us that there's more to it than that. Wherever men put him, whatever they did with him, Paul would find a way of telling others about his Master. "We've locked him up in jail; that will silence him!" the Roman authorities thought. The next thing they knew was that the jailers (the Praetorian guards) were being converted!

And note that others were encouraged by his witness (14). Everyone, anywhere, can spread the Good News. All we need is to know Christ for ourselves and to tell others what he means to us.

*Christ proclaimed with ignoble motives (15-18).* What a strange thing! People were busy preaching the gospel, not simply because they wanted to bring others to Christ, but because they wanted to embarrass Paul. (They would slip into their preaching some remarks which criticized him and his teaching.) Note Paul's attitude to all this (18). Of course, he doesn't recommend it, but he sees some value in it. It's all too easy to criticize other people's methods or even be envious of their results. But if the Good News about Jesus is being spread, we should rejoice.

### My Response

### Memory Point

Keep reading Key Verse 7 (Phil. 2:5-8) aloud until you are able to say it three times in a row without making a mistake.

### ☐ PRAY to apply God's Word

Ask God to give you one opportunity to proclaim Christ today . . .

# 33

☐ **PRAY for insight into God's Word**
Father, I willingly release to you now all the preoccupations on my mind. I want to hear your voice.

☐ **READ Philippians 1:19-30**

☐ **MEDITATE on God's Word**

*Discovery*
**1.** What seems to be a possible consequence of Paul's imprisonment (20)? What is his attitude toward this possibility (21–23)?

_____

_____

**2.** What is Paul's understanding of God's will for his life (22, 24)? How does this help him cope with his life-threatening situation (25–26)? What lesson do you find here?

_____

_____

_____

**3.** What uncomfortable truth does Paul reveal about the Christian life (29)? Do you think this is or should be the norm for all Christians today? Why or why not?

_____

_____

_____

_____

**4.** How do you feel about your own death? Does Paul's example (21–23) help you? If so, how?

_____

_____

_____

_____

### Reflection

Fear is one of the biggest hindrances to Christian joy and to the spread of the gospel. But Paul had two ways of showing how to live a life free of fear.

*His life (19-26).* Looked at from the outside, Paul was powerless and threatened; he might be put to death at any time, and he had absolutely no security. But looked at from the inside, Paul was invulnerable, beyond being hurt. How could this be? It was because he was living "in Christ" and "for Christ" and "with Christ." So, if he lived he could introduce others to Christ; if he was killed he would be in the presence of Christ forever (20-21).

Christians living under persecution in many countries today have learned to live in just the same spirit. Those of us who live in comfortable circumstances find it very much harder, but it is not impossible. A major part is deciding what things really give us security.

*His teaching (27-30).* Paul didn't want the Philippians, or us, to be afraid of anything (28). The secret is:
—unity in the one fellowship ("one spirit" 27).
—sharing in the one task ("contending as one man" 27).
—trusting in the one Deliverer ("without being frightened in any way" 28).
—"going through the same struggle" (30), that is, being willing to suffer, if necessary, in the battle against Satan and sin. Paul was pointing out the need for unity if we are to live in a way that is worthy of Christians.

### My Response

### Memory Point

Review Key Verse 7 (Phil. 2:5-8) several times. Then face yourself in a mirror, look at your eyes and say the passage aloud.

### ☐ PRAY to apply God's Word

What is your greatest fear in life? What is your greatest fear about sharing the gospel? Talk to God about both of these today . . .

# 34

□ **PRAY for insight into God's Word**

"What language shall I borrow to thank thee, dearest friend, for this thy dying sorrow, thy pity without end? O make me thine forever; and should I fainting be, Lord, let me never, never outlive my love to thee" *(Bernard of Clairvaux).*

□ **READ Philippians 2:1-11**

□ **MEDITATE on God's Word**

*Discovery*

**1.** In five words or less (ones different from those used in the text) summarize what Paul is asking the Philippian Christians to do (2). What is the secret to accomplishing this (3-4)?

_____

_____

_____

**2.** Write down the names of the three people with whom you associate closely. Now list one way you could put verses 3 and 4 into action with these people this month.

_____

_____

_____

**3.** Reread verses 5-11 several times. What *new* things do you learn about Jesus?

_____

_____

_____

**4.** In what way do you most want to become like Christ? How might you begin accomplishing this goal today?

_____

_____

_____

### Reflection

One fundamental principle of Christianity is that belief *must* affect behavior. Jesus emphasized it (John 14:15). James emphasized it (James 1:22). John emphasized it (1 John 4:20). And so does Paul in this very famous passage.

*Christian behavior (1-5).* Among the problems of the church at Philippi was a tendency to quarrel. Two women Paul mentions in 4:2 were examples of this. Paul's teaching is clear: Christians are what they are only because they have experienced the love of God (1). Nobody has any reason to boast or to judge others. Rather, we should look for positive ways of helping each other (4).

*Christian belief (6-11).* Most religions and philosophies have something to say about loving your neighbor—or, at least, not hurting him. But Christianity has something special and distinctive—the example of Jesus Christ. So Paul clearly explains Christ's nature in order to emphasize his call for loving behavior:

—*Who Jesus is (6-8):* "in very nature God" and "equal with God" are both ways of saying that he is God (6). In the same way, words like "the form of a servant" and "human likeness" (7) teach us that he became truly and fully a man.

—*What Jesus will be (9-11):* the day will come when he will be revealed as Lord of all—so the nearer we get to obeying his will now, the happier that day will be for us.

### My Response

### Memory Point

If you watch TV or listen to the radio today, use all the time for commercials to mentally or verbally repeat Key Verse 7 (Phil. 2:5-8).

### ☐ PRAY to apply God's Word

As you pray today, look up (towards the sky if possible) and thank Jesus aloud for all he means to you . . .

# 35

☐ **PRAY for insight into God's Word**

Holy Spirit, I want to know you. I want to hear you speaking clearly to me from this passage. Let my time today be more than just a routine study. I want to meet you now, so please make me sensitive to how you are going to do this.

☐ **READ Philippians 2:12–18**

☐ **MEDITATE on God's Word**

### Discovery

**1.** In what sense do you think Paul meant "work out your salvation" (12)? How could this verse be misused? How does verse 13 establish a proper understanding of verse 12?

_____

_____

_____

*Note: work out your own salvation (12)—"To work out one's own eternal welfare or salvation does not mean that man can or must work and accomplish it himself, for God does that (13); but the believer must finish, must carry to conclusion, must apply to its fullest consequence, what is already given by God in principle. . . . He must 'work out' what God in his grace has 'worked in.'" (Jac J. Muller, The Epistles of Paul to the Philippians and to Philemon, The New International Commentary on the New Testament [Eerdmans, 1955], p. 91).*

**2.** What do the words "fear and trembling" in verse 12 suggest? (If possible, read verses 12–18 in several different Bible translations.) How could you become more serious about your relationship with Jesus?

_____

_____

**3.** What is the significance of the word "everything" in verse 14? Is it possible to obey this command?

_____

_____

**4.** In what ways are you a light (15) in your world? What causes your light to become dim? What makes it become brighter?

_____

_____

_____

## Reflection

Paul now spells out what follows from the truth that Christ is to be Lord of all (9–11) in two short phrases.

*"Work out"* *(12)*. This verse does not mean that we must somehow save ourselves, or that we are left to our own devices as Christians. Our job is to make our bodies as fit and strong as they can be. That is the sense here. We are to show in our behavior and our attitudes that we are God's children (15). As we do so, people will see in us the sort of life that God looks for.

Verse 14 gives one example of what this will mean. But "complaining" and "arguing" are still common faults among Christians. No matter how mature in Christ we have become we can view this verse as a daily challenge.

"Fear and trembling" doesn't mean being afraid that God will punish or abandon us; it means "Keep in mind that great day when Jesus will be Lord of all, and your life will be seen in its true value—as he sees it."

*"Works in you"* *(13)*. This is the secret behind all genuine Christian living— God's Holy Spirit is continually strengthening and helping us. We have our part to play ("work out"); he will certainly do his ("work in").

Paul wants to be proud of the Philippians when he meets Christ (16), and that reminds him that he may be killed at any moment. But he sees that as a small price to pay for the Philippians' conversion. So he wants them to be glad with him.

## My Response

## Memory Point

Think of a Christian friend you will see today (or that you could call). When you do, say, "Here's the word for you today . . ." and repeat Key Verse 7 (Phil. 2:5–8).

## ☐ PRAY to apply God's Word

Confess to your Father the areas you are most prone to complain or argue. Then ask him to renew your attitudes in these matters . . .

# 36

☐ **PRAY for insight into God's Word**
Spend a few minutes worshiping the living God before you begin your study.

☐ **READ Philippians 2:19-30**

☐ **MEDITATE on God's Word**

*Discovery*
**1.** Why was Paul planning to send Timothy to Philippi (19)? Why was Timothy so valuable to Paul (20-24)?

_____

_____

**2.** Why was Epaphroditus with Paul (25 and 4:18)? Why was Paul sending him to Philippi (28)?

_____

_____

_____

**3.** How could you become less concerned for your own interests and more concerned for those of Jesus in the coming year (21)? Try to be specific. Are there any dangers or traps in self-sacrifice?

_____

_____

_____

_____

**4.** Epaphroditus risked his life for God's work (30). What risks (not necessarily physical) could you take to advance the cause of Christ in your home, neighborhood or work environment?

_____

_____

_____

### Reflection

Paul now shared news of two coworkers he planned to send to the Philippians. In his view they were imitators of Christ and exemplified some of the virtues and qualities he had described earlier in the letter.

*Timothy (19-24).* This young man was not a self-centered individual. He had a genuine concern for the church at Philippi (20), for the work of Christ (22), and for the welfare of Paul (22). This outward-looking spirit is a challenge to all believers at a time when selfish materialism and loveless indifference are all around. Note what Paul said: "I have no one like him." Can the minister or leader at your local church say that about you? It is because of the unselfish service of such people throughout the centuries that Christ's work has been maintained and extended.

*Epaphroditus (25-30).* This man (mentioned only in this letter) was the messenger from the Philippians; he brought their gift to Paul, and the journey seems to have involved him in serious hazards (30). This section of the letter indicates the value the apostle put on his close Christian friends. It is all too easy for us to become insular and self-sufficient, failing to recognize the immense debt we owe to other Christians. Think today with gratitude of those who first brought the gospel to our land, those who first shared the Good News with you personally and who, by word and example, make it easier for you to maintain your faith in Jesus.

### My Response

### Memory Point

What have you learned by memorizing Key Verse 7 (Phil. 2:5-8)?

### ☐ PRAY to apply God's Word

Pray for the Christians you know who have devoted themselves to full-time Christian service . . .

# 8/Philippians 3:1–4:23
# Living for the Lord

☐ **Introduction**

In a conversation where a person is trying to explain something important, he will carefully spell out the facts in a logical order. But to be sure he has communicated he will stop at various stages of the explanation and ask, "Do you understand what I mean?" If the listener hesitates or simply says, "Well . . . not really," he goes back and attempts to communicate the same message using a different approach, new words, and other explanations. That's what Paul is doing in chapters 3 and 4 of Philippians.

In the first half of the epistle, Paul focused on a vitally important concept: imitating Christ. It was so important that he wants to make sure no one misses the point. So in the second half of his letter, he writes about the same basic theme using a different approach. After finishing chapter two, we can almost hear Paul say, "Wait a minute, let me explain what I mean in a different way."

Paul changes pace by focusing on the lordship of Jesus Christ. In fact, he uses the term "Lord" seven times in these two chapters and connects it to some very practical instructions: "stand firm in the Lord"; "agree in the Lord"; "rejoice in the Lord." Indeed, another way to imitate Christ is to attempt to make Jesus lord of every aspect of life.

Paul picks out several unrelated areas of daily life where he is especially concerned that the Philippian Christians apply the lordship of Christ. If you approach your next readings with this theme in mind, you will hear Paul saying, "You can succeed at living for the Lord by . . ."

*Rejoicing (3:1).* Even though he is writing from inside a Roman prison, while false teachers on the outside are aggressively trying to undermine all the work he has done, Paul is bursting with the joy of the Lord. He uses the term for rejoicing sixteen times in the letter.

*Pressing on (3:14).* Paul is like a champion marathon runner. He is tempted by the desire to fade into the background or to quit, but he never gives in. He strains to do his best in the Lord's service to the very end of his life.

*Agreeing (4:2).* Two women, who seem to have been influential people in the Philippian church, had gotten into some major quarrel. Making Jesus Lord meant these two women must put an end to the argument.

*Giving (4:10–19).* Paul takes time to graciously acknowledge a contribution the Philippians had made to him. In so doing he communicates the secret of contentment.

*Remaining anxiety-free (4:6–7).* An unshakable sense of peace should characterize a Christian's life. And Paul explains how. First, by trusting God's sovereignty (1:6; 4:19). Second, by earnestly praying (4:6–7).

*Developing a rich thought life (4:8–9).* Paul didn't disengage his mind when he accepted Christ and neither should we. Christians should have active minds whether we've had a lot of schooling or not. Paul gives a whole list of ways we can develop one.

*Rejoicing even more (4:4).* Paul can't say enough about this subject. He returns to it several times. Christians should learn to genuinely rejoice now since it will be one of our main activities for eternity.

Of course Paul's list is not exhaustive. There are plenty of other ways to make Jesus lord. And Paul would never want anyone to think that the way to God was by fulfilling some list of do's and don'ts. The way to God is by faith in Jesus Christ alone. But having accepted Christ, the way to live is to become preoccupied with making him lord of all.

☐ **Key Verse 8: Philippians 4:4–7**
Rejoice in the Lord always. I will say it again: Rejoice! Let your gentleness be evident to all. The Lord is near. Do not be anxious about anything, but in everything, by prayer and petition, with thanksgiving, present your requests to God. And the peace of God, which transcends all understanding, will guard your hearts and your minds in Christ Jesus.

☐ **Outline**

*Philippians: Paths to Joy*

I.  Imitating Christ
    A. Thanksgiving and prayer  *1:1–11*
    B. Paul's example  *1:12–30*
    C. The humility of Christ  *2:1–18*
    D. Timothy and Epaphroditus  *2:19–30*

II. **Living for the Lord**
    A. **New priorities**  *3:1–11*
    B. **Pressing on**  *3:12–21*
    C. **Rejoicing**  *4:1–13*
    D. **Acknowledging a gift**  *4:14–23*

# 37

☐ **PRAY for insight into God's Word**
Lord, help me to forget about the concerns and pressures of my life so that I may single-mindedly concentrate on you.

☐ **READ Philippians 3:1-11**

☐ **MEDITATE on God's Word**

*Discovery*
1. How specifically do you obey Paul's command in verse 1a?

_____

_____

**2.** What happens to Paul's attitude between verses 1 and 2? What is his chief complaint against the people he has in mind in verses 2-6? How do you react to those who misrepresent the gospel?

_____

_____

**3.** Carefully reexamine the various clauses of verses 7-11. Then answer these questions:
**a.** What gives you your deepest fellowship with Jesus?

_____

_____

**b.** In what way have you experienced the greatest measure of God's power?

_____

_____

**c.** Are you eager to suffer for Christ as Paul was? Why?

_____

_____

**d.** What makes you certain you will have eternal life?

_____

_____

### Reflection

In Paul's day there were professing Christians who taught that Gentiles must become Jews before becoming Christians. They taught a false gospel. It was faith in Christ, plus Judaism. Paul always opposed them severely (2, 18–19; Gal. 1:8–9). Similar dangers face us today when anyone teaches that we need to have Christianity plus something else. No wonder Paul tells us that Christ himself is enough because in him we may find everything necessary for salvation. He then turns from the divisive activities of these legalistic teachers to his own experience (4).

*What he left (5–8).* As Paul adds each item to this long list of his religious, social and moral attainments (Gal. 1:14), he may be presenting a deliberate contrast— the arrogant, self-centered man described here versus the humble, self-renouncing Christ portrayed in the previous chapter (2:5–11). Far from being helpful, Paul's previous distinctions were actually hindrances; they created and helped to sustain a proud self-confidence that caused him to rely on his own achievements rather than on grace alone.

*What he gained (9).* Abandoning his self-righteousness, he came to depend solely on Christ. He left the works of the law as a means of salvation and was brought to utter reliance upon the work of Christ. Righteousness comes from God, through Christ and by faith (9).

*What he desires (10–11).* Paul now has entirely different spiritual ambitions. He wants to know Christ in a deeper personal relationship, experience his power, enter into his sufferings, and share his ultimate assured victory. Is that true of you as well?

### My Response

### Memory Point

Write out Key Verse 8 (Phil. 4:4–7) on a 3x5 card and tape or place it in a familiar spot. Throughout the day, whenever you see it, repeat the verse several times.

### ☐ PRAY to apply God's Word

Ask for God's power in the area of your Christian life where you feel weakest . . .

# 38

**PRAY for insight into God's Word**

Father, I am hungry to know more about you. Please satisfy me today.

☐ **READ Philippians 3:12–21**

☐ **MEDITATE on God's Word**

*Discovery*

**1.** How is the apostle's humility evident (12–13)? Why is it important that Paul communicate this to his readers (17)?

_____

_____

**2.** Who does Paul feel is responsible for his own salvation (12b)? Is this also true for you?

_____

**3.** List some areas of your Christian life where you need to "forget" and "press on" (13–14). Now jot down how you could do so in each case.

_____

_____

_____

_____

**4.** What mistake had some of the Philippians made (18–19)? How are twentieth-century Christians susceptible to the temptations and dangers of hedonism? How do these dangers ensnare you?

_____

_____

_____

_____

## Reflection

In these verses, Paul shares three principles that helped him face the challenges and difficulties of being an apostle. You'll do well to follow them as well, no matter what life situation God has given you.

*"Forgetting" (13).* We all know that the past cannot just be dismissed out of hand; we are all affected by childhood experiences, sufferings , and the influence of others. Nor did Paul literally "forget" his past (see 3:5-6; also 1 Cor. 15:9). So what does he mean by "forgetting"? We must not allow any sin or failure from the past to hinder our freedom and confidence in Christ now. We should not rest on the achievements of the past but move on. We must not be satisfied with yesterday's experience of Christ but must look for a living relationship now.

*"Straining forward" (13 RSV).* Salvation is a free gift; the Holy Spirit indwells us to give us strength to follow Christ. So why does Paul have to make such an effort? His description suggests an athlete driving himself for the finish. Look back to verse 12. "To make it my own" and "Jesus has made me his own" (RSV) suggest a two-way process. We receive God's gifts, but we are responsible for making full use of them.

*Waiting (20).* We are all far from perfect, and the world is certainly in a mess. But Christians do not despair, for we look forward to the return of Jesus Christ when our bodies and spirits will be made perfect.

## My Response

## Memory Point

Read Key Verse 8 (Phil. 4:4-7) aloud until you can say it three times without error. Also, plan to set your alarm clock ten minutes early and go over the verses first thing tomorrow.

## ☐ PRAY to apply God's Word

Think of the ways you sometimes give in to the hedonistic pressures around you. Ask God to forgive you and make you a more disciplined servant of his . . .

# 39

☐ **PRAY for insight into God's Word**
Raising your hands, look up and sing the Doxology (or other familiar hymn of praise).

☐ **READ Philippians 4:1-7**

☐ **MEDITATE on God's Word**

*Discovery*
**1.** What three directives does Paul attach to the phrase "in the Lord" (1-2, 4)? What significance do you see in this?

_____

_____

_____

**2.** Think of some individual Christians or groups you know who are currently at odds. What is your responsibility to them (2-3)?

_____

_____

**3.** How does Paul advise the Philippians (and you) to react to life's problems (6)? What is the result of such action (7)? In what ways do you need to act on these verses now?

_____

_____

_____

_____

**4.** Why do you think rejoicing is so vital to living the Christian life (4)?

_____

_____

_____

### Reflection

Everyone, it seems, is searching for peace. The problem is, not many find it. But Paul points out in these verses that it shouldn't be like that for Christians and he tells us exactly what to do about it.

*Peace in the church (2-3).* It is a tragedy when Christians quarrel. It can undo all the good we may have done in our work for the gospel. Where differences exist we should not simply ignore them. We should do all we can to bring real peace and understanding. Instead of being rough and resentful we should be gentle (5). The Lord is close by and will see that justice is done.

*Peace in the heart (6-7).* Very often we are at odds with other people because we are not at peace in ourselves. So the inner peace in verse 6 is important both for the church and for the individuals in it:

—*Negative*—"do not be anxious": this was Jesus' own teaching (Matt 6:25-33).
—*Positive*—"in everything . . . by prayer . . . with thanksgiving." Prayer means first that we commit ourselves, our lives, and our loved ones into God's hands without any reserve or limitation; it is an act of total trust. We may ask for certain things as we pray, but this is always within the framework of his overriding will.

When we trust God like this we will find complete security. We will also find a new joy. There can be no real joy when we are worried, but trusting in the Lord will enable us to be joyful even when circumstances seem against it.

### My Response

### Memory Point

Before you sit down for any meal today, practice Key Verse 8 (Phil. 4:4-7) until you can say it at least once without a mistake.

### ☐ PRAY to apply God's Word

Think of the three things that are causing the most anxiety for you now. Visualize yourself holding them inside your two clenched fists. Then open your hands, palms up, and imagine yourself presenting them to God, as verse 6 says, and claim the promise of verse 7 as you release them to him.

# 40

□ **PRAY for insight into God's Word**
"Grant me, Lord, to know all that I should know, to love what I should love, to esteem what pleases you, and to reject all that is evil in your sight. Let me . . . discern between things spiritual and material, and seek your will and good pleasure at all times and above all else" *(Thomas à Kempis)*.

□ **READ Philippians 4:8-13**

□ **MEDITATE on God's Word**

*Discovery*
**1.** For five of the categories Paul cites in verse 8, list the most poignant example from your experience.

_____

_____

_____

_____

_____

**2.** What do you think was Paul's motive for his instruction in verse 8? How does verse 9 further accomplish that motive?

_____

_____

**3.** Of the two living situations Paul mentions in verse 12, which are you in now? Can you honestly say to God that you'd be willing *and happy* to accept the other alternative? What makes you think so?

_____

_____

_____

**4.** What is the secret to a genuinely positive attitude (13)? How could you demonstrate this attitude in the next week?

_____

_____

## Reflection

Do you know people who talk and act as if the Christian life really made them happy? Well, that's the way it should be for all Christians! Look again at verses 7, 9b, 13 and 19. God is not mocking us here with promises he will not keep. And it is all for here and now.

Why then, are there so many Christians who are negative, down, and depressed? Paul's teaching and example once again challenge us.

*Do we control our thoughts (8)?* Through what we hear and see we are bombarded with things which tempt us to envy, jealousy, impatience, hatred, covetousness, lust, and unbelief. We cannot avoid temptation altogether. But there is something very positive we can do (8).

*Do we accept difficulties (11)?* The words "I have learned" in verses 11 and 12 are encouraging; they suggest that Paul hadn't always found it easy to be content. Yet he was in situations far more difficult than we shall probably ever experience. (See 2 Cor. 11:23–29.)

*Do we know how to live if the way is easy (12, 18)?* David did so well when the way was hard—for example, in sparing Saul's life (1 Sam. 26:8–9). But he went sadly wrong when life was easy in his palace (2 Sam. 1:1–15). Paul has set us a good example for "whatever state" we are in.

## My Response

## Memory Point

Whenever you are walking alone, at home, at work or outside, say Key Verse 8 (Phil. 4:4–7) aloud.

## ☐ PRAY to apply God's Word

Ask God to give you a renewed confidence in him and the opportunity to share it with others today.

# *41*

□ **PRAY for insight into God's Word**
Dear Lord, help me to see how these verses call me to action today.

□ **READ Philippians 4:14–23**

□ **MEDITATE on God's Word**

*Discovery*
**1.** What fact about the Philippian church does Paul especially note (15)? What does this indicate about them?

_____

_____

**2.** Characterize Paul's attitude toward the gifts he received (17–20). What principles do you see here to guide those who handle or use the financial gifts of other Christians?

_____

_____

_____

**3.** What motivates you to contribute money to your church or a Christian ministry? What are good and bad reasons for giving? How could you demonstrate leadership in supporting some area of God's work this year?

_____

_____

_____

**4.** What are your greatest needs right now? How does verse 19 relate to these needs? What is the difference between wanting and needing something?

_____

_____

_____

_____

### Reflection

It is not as easy to accept the help of others as we may think; it means that we have to admit our need and our dependence, and this may hurt our pride. Although he had learned how to cope with things like hunger and want, Paul did not make himself independent of those who wanted to help him. So when the Philippian Christians three times sent him gifts—first when he had just left them, then when he was in Thessalonica, and finally when he was in Rome—he accepted their help thankfully and graciously. He saw such giving for what it really was.

*A fragrant offering (18).* This is the language of the Old Testament, where the Jews brought their regular offerings to God and burned their incense in the tabernacle and the temple. Such offerings are no longer dictated by God's law; in their place are the loving gifts which show that we Christians specially care for one another.

*An acceptable sacrifice (18).* This is Old Testament language again. Since Jesus offered himself on the cross, no further sacrifices are necessary or valid. Instead we are called to be priests and we can all offer sacrifices as we help to meet the needs of others. Such giving brings pleasure to God.

### My Response

### Memory Point

What part of Key Verse 8 (Phil. 4:4-7) is the most meaningful to you?

### ☐ PRAY to apply God's Word

Refer to your answer to question 4 on the previous page. Talk to God about these concerns now . . .

# 9/Colossians 1:1–3:4
# Correction for Error

## ☐ Introduction
(For a helpful overview of Paul's letter to the Colossians, review the material found on page 11 of this book.)

Preparing a balance sheet for a large company is a detailed and important job. Many figures and bits of information must be collected. Cash on hand, accounts receivable, savings, inventory totals, equipment value, investments, accounts payable and loans outstanding are just a few of the facts necessary in order to begin the job.

Companies often use computers to help them develop a balance sheet faster. Of course, using a computer does not eliminate the possibility of error. If the original data was incorrect, or if the data was correct but improperly entered into the computer, the balance sheet will be wrong. A small mistake made at the early stages will often be compounded by the computer's automated calculations into colossal errors throughout the entire balance sheet, making it unusable.

If such errors occur, the balance sheet must be given to financial experts. Their job is to spot where the error occurred and to determine what must be done to correct it.

The apostle Paul had received a "spiritual balance sheet" from one of his associates, Epaphras, summarizing the condition of the churches in and around Colosse (Colossae). From what Epaphras reported, Paul, like a trained financial expert, was able to spot some incipient theological errors that had developed. And since the church in Colosse was relatively young, Paul wanted to correct them before they mushroomed into destructive heresies.

Since Paul had never visited Colosse and had never met his readers, his letter lacks the personal quality of some of his other epistles. In fact, some sections of Colossians are rather terse. Paul was cordial and concerned, but his focus was on the business of correcting the errors he had spotted, as you will see in your next several readings.

The first two chapters of Colossians present us with a strategy for helping others who are contemplating false ideas about Christianity. First, Paul praised his readers for their positive characteristics (1:3–8); for the faith, love, and hope which they had demonstrated. Even though there were problems in this church, Paul kept them in perspective. He tactfully began by letting the Colossians know he hadn't forgotten all the good things about them.

Second, he prayed for their spiritual growth (1:9-14). Paul knew that you couldn't have a healthy church by simply rooting out errors. You had to be making spiritual progress forward as well.

Third, he focused on Christ (1:15). In so doing, he wrote one of the richest theological explanations of Jesus Christ in the entire New Testament. Paul believed the best way to correct errors was to know Jesus better and better.

Fourth, Paul reported some details about his own situation; his suffering, struggle, and work for the name of Christ. Although they had never met, Paul didn't want the Colossians to question his sincerity.

Finally, Paul tackled the errors he had heard about. After winning their respect and establishing the supremacy of Christ, he was able to erase the errors with ease and put his readers back on the right track.

After examining this positive strategy, however, you may be tempted to think, "How come Paul dealt with the false teaching in Galatia by getting angry but in Colosse by being 'Mr. Positive'? How can *I* know which approach to take?"

The answer lies in analyzing his readers. In Galatians Paul was angry at the false *teachers*, the ones who were deliberately leading others astray. In Colossians he was positive and tolerant with the members of the congregation, the ones who were listening, and even accepting, but not officially promoting, false doctrine.

Understanding that distinction could save Christians today much unnecessary division. The church desperately needs not only men and women who will firmly stand against those who preach heresy and false doctrine, but also those who will tolerantly and patiently stay with a church and help those who are confused or weak in faith to more clearly understand the gospel of Jesus Christ.

☐ **Key Verse 9: Colossians 1:19-20**

For God was pleased to have all his fullness dwell in him, and through him to reconcile to himself all things, whether things on earth or things in heaven, by making peace through his blood, shed on the cross.

☐ **Outline**

*Colossians: Focus on Christ*

I. **Correction for Error**
   A. **Thanksgiving and prayer** *1:1-14*
   B. **Description of Christ** *1:15-23*
   C. **Paul's situation** *1:24-2:7*
   D. **Erasing errors** *2:8-3:4*

II. **Directions for Living**
   A. Old and new habits *3:5-17*
   B. Christian households *3:18-4:1*
   C. Instructions and greetings *4:2-18*

# 42

☐ **PRAY for insight into God's Word**
Dear Lord, help me to listen carefully for your living voice as I begin this study of Colossians.

☐ **READ Colossians 1:1-8**

☐ **MEDITATE on God's Word**

*Discovery*
**1.** What does the phrase "we have heard of " (4) seem to indicate about Paul's relationship with his readers? How had the Colossians heard the gospel (7-8)?

_____

_____

**2.** What two things about the Colossians does Paul thank God for (3-5)? To what does Paul attribute these traits (5)?

_____

_____

**3.** What effect was the gospel having (6)? How have you seen this same phenomenon happening in your church within the last year?

_____

_____

_____

**4.** How did you first hear the gospel? What caused you to accept it? How is the gospel bearing fruit in your life now?

_____

_____

_____

_____

### Reflection

As we begin this magnificent letter we immediately learn some things about its receivers and its sender.

*Receivers: God's people in Colosse.* Colosse was one of the churches in Asia Minor that Paul himself had not founded. Its biggest problem was caused by men who claimed to be Christian teachers, but who were saying that Jesus Christ was only one—though the chief one—of a series of heavenly beings who made up a kind of chain of communication between man and God. False teachers have always been active in the church; they are busy today. We should learn how to deal with them as we study this epistle.

*Sender: God's servant in prison.* Paul had plenty of problems of his own—he was in prison in Rome, awaiting trial, and possibly a death sentence. But notice how a Christian should deal with trouble:

—*He heard (4, 8).* He did not spend all his time grumbling about his own problem; he thought of his friends and of other Christians "all over the world" (6).

—*He gave thanks (3).* He was "praying always," KJV (3). His body was confined to prison; his spirit traveled the world in prayer. Sometimes the best way to deal with our own trouble is to be absorbed in caring for others.

### My Response

### Memory Point

Write Key Verse 9 (Col. 1:19–20) on a 3x5 card and place it in a familiar spot. Whenever you see the card throughout the day, repeat the verse several times.

### ☐ PRAY to apply God's Word

Pray for the Christian who first introduced you to the gospel (or thank God for that person) . . .

# 43

☐ **PRAY for insight into God's Word**
"Renew my life, O Lord, according to your word!" (Ps. 119:107).

☐ **READ Colossians 1:9–14**

☐ **MEDITATE on God's Word**

*Discovery*
**1.** Paul's prayer (9–14) contains three requests of God and one suggestion to the Colossians. Find and summarize each in your own words.
Request #1 (9)

_____

Request #2 (10)

_____

Request #3 (11)

_____

Suggestion (12–14)

_____

**2.** List the facts about salvation that are either stated or implied in verses 12–14.

_____

_____

_____

**3.** Which of Paul's three requests for the Colossians is most appropriate for you? Why? How could you help answer that request? How could you seek the help of fellow Christians to answer it?

_____

_____

_____

_____

### Reflection

Paul had not visited Colosse—but he was often there in his prayers. Note what he prays for: it outlines a program for Christian living:

*Knowledge of God's will (9).* Note that this is not just head-knowledge, or human wisdom. It is "spiritual"; that is, it is given by God's Spirit to receptive Christians.

*Living in God's way (10).* This is made up of several parts—obedience, which pleases him; good works, which are the "fruit" of his presence; and a growing understanding of what God is like—all these bring us nearer to him.

*Made strong with God's power (11).* The purpose of this power is not to help us to do spectacular miracles; it is rather to help us to endure and be patient. We don't usually think so much about this kind of virtue—but it's a sign of strength when we can endure and even suffer patiently and joyfully.

*Acknowledging God's favor (12).* Usually when we talk of someone being "qualified" we refer to their ability and their achievement; but here, notice, it is God who "qualifies" us. How? Through the work of his Son on the Cross (13–14).

### My Response

### Memory Point

Repeat Key Verse 9 (Col. 1:19–20) until you can confidently say it without looking.

### ☐ PRAY to apply God's Word

Pray for the Christian with whom you most closely associate using the topics Paul used in his prayer (9–14) . . .

# 44

☐ **PRAY for insight into God's Word**

Lord Jesus, I want to know you better. I want to know that you are real and alive and that you are actually with me right now. Please give me a deeper fellowship with you through my study and prayer today.

☐ **READ Colossians 1:15–23**

☐ **MEDITATE on God's Word**

*Discovery*

**1.** Which truth about Jesus in Paul's description (15–20) seems most important to you? Why?

_____

_____

**2.** What new things do you learn about Jesus from these verses?

_____

_____

*Note: He is the image of the invisible God (15–20)—"In view of the great stress Paul places on Christology in this Epistle, it is reasonable to suppose that the false teaching was defective in this respect. Any view of Christ which denied him the pre-eminence in everything (cf. 1:18) would be inferior to Paul's view of him. Indeed it is a fair inference that the exalted view of Christ set out in the whole section 1:15–20 was called out by the opposite tendencies of the false teachers" (Donald Guthrie, The New Bible Commentary: Revised, Colossians [Eerdmans, 1970], p. 1140).*

**3.** What does the word "reconciled" (20, 22) teach you about the nature of salvation? (If possible, check a dictionary.) What responsibility do you have in regard to reconciliation with God (23)?

_____

_____

_____

**4.** What is the "hope of the gospel" (23)? When are you tempted to lose your hope? What truth from this passage could help you not to lose hope?

_____

_____

## Reflection

Now Paul focuses his attention on Jesus Christ as a way of countering the wrong teaching in Colosse. The errors there took two forms. One erroneous teaching was that Christ was not really divine, but simply one among many wonderful beings. Another was that Christians were not really saved, but still needed to work hard to achieve their salvation. Paul tackles both errors right here in these 9 verses.

*He—the Christ (15).* Do you have too small an opinion of Jesus Christ? Let verses 15-20 help your perspective: He is God made visible, Master of everything created, completely sufficient Redeemer, and Governor of his church.

*And you—the Christian (21).* First, see where you started (21)—far from God in position, thoughts, and actions. Now see the wonderful difference Christ has made—you are reconciled, and without blame in God's sight (22). And he demands no effort or payment—just that you keep faith with him (23).

## My Response

## Memory Point

Look up Key Verse 9 (Col. 1:19-20) in as many different Bible versions as you can. Which do you like best? Why?

## ☐ PRAY to apply God's Word

Use a different-than-usual prayer position (kneeling, standing, looking up) and worship Jesus in your time of prayer . . .

# 45

☐ **PRAY for insight into God's Word**

"Oh, how I love your law! I meditate on it all day long" (Ps. 119:97).

☐ **READ Colossians 1:24-29**

☐ **MEDITATE on God's Word**

*Discovery*

**1.** What was Paul's situation as he wrote (24)? What was his attitude toward it?

_____

_____

*Note: I complete what is lacking in Christ's afflictions (24)—"The sense in which the suffering and death of Christ have won justification and reconciliation for men is unique, unrepeatable. . . . But in the sense in which Paul intends here, Christ continues to suffer in his members, and not least in Paul himself. This truth was impressed on Paul's mind in the very moment of his conversion when he heard the voice of Christ say, "Why persecutest thou me?" (F. F. Bruce, The Epistle to the Ephesians and Colossians, The New International Commentary on the New Testament [Eerdmans, 1957], p. 216).*

**2.** What mission was Paul attempting to accomplish (24-25, 28-29)?

_____

_____

**3.** What is the mystery to which Paul referred (26-27)? What evidence demonstrates that Christ is in you?

_____

_____

_____

**4.** Have you ever suffered for the sake of other Christians? When, and how did you feel about doing it? In what specific way could you risk suffering now for the sake of other Christians?

_____

_____

_____

## Reflection

Today's reading reveals the essence of the Christian life in two short phrases. Note that in both cases, the focus is on Christ.

"*Christ in you*" (27). Paul describes this as a "mystery." He does not mean that it is something which cannot be understood; in his time "explaining a mystery" meant to interpret clearly something which had previously been obscure. Obviously, the gospel could not have been properly known before Jesus Christ himself had lived and died and risen again. But now, as Paul went around preaching, it became what we might call an open secret. There are many people in the world today to whom it is still a mystery in every sense. Are you doing what you can to remove the darkness from their minds?

"Christ in you" is the shortest possible way of describing what it means to be a Christian. Outwardly you are alive as much as before. But there is a tremendous difference—in you is Christ, who has already been described to us in verses 15-20; he lives in you!

"*Perfect in Christ*" (28). This does not contradict the previous idea; it adds to it and completes it—it is the other side of the coin. It is the Christian's life—as God sees it. He sees us as holy and righteous and all that we ought to be because he sees us in Christ. We are accepted and forgiven and welcomed for Christ's sake, not because we ourselves are perfect.

## My Response

## Memory Point

Put your 3x5 card with Key Verse 9 (Col. 1:19-20) on it in your wallet or purse. Whenever you spend money today, review the verse.

## ☐ PRAY to apply God's Word

Ask the Holy Spirit for courage to help you act on what you have answered in question 4, using the first opportunity you have . . .

# 46

☐ **PRAY for insight into God's Word**
Hold your hands out, palms up, and ask the Holy Spirit to fill you with insight as you think about God's Word today.

☐ **READ Colossians 2:1-7**

☐ **MEDITATE on God's Word**

*Discovery*
**1.** What does Paul say is the most important thing for these Christians to know (2-3)? What is included in this "knowledge"?

_____

_____

**2.** Why was Paul concerned about the Colossians' faith (4)? What are some examples of this type of danger today?

_____

_____

_____

**3.** How could Paul's instructions in verses 6-7 help the Colossians keep their faith from swerving?

_____

_____

_____

**4.** Identify a new Christian who needs someone to protect and encourage his or her budding faith. In what ways could you help this person?

_____

_____

_____

## Reflection

The apostle Paul was responsible for so many groups of new Christians that it must have been difficult for him to care genuinely about each one. Yet today's reading shows how deeply concerned he was that these Colossian Christians (whom he had never seen) continue to grow in Christ.

*Paul's concern:* "I strive for you" (1, RSV); "I am with you" (5, RSV). How did he strive? His exertion was a spiritual struggle of prayer. "Strive" indicates the level of exertion found in a hard wrestling match. Think about the way we pray for others. Do we bother to find out what their needs are? Do we read missionary news carefully? And how was Paul "present with them in spirit" (5)? He entered into their situation, making the effort to find out exactly what was happening to them, and then imaginatively sharing their experience with them. You and I have Christian brothers and sisters in other lands who are in prison for the sake of the gospel; do we ever get within a thousand miles of being "with" them like that?

*Paul's command:* "As you received . . . so live . . ." (6, RSV). Already the members of this young church were in danger of being led astray by false teaching; Paul's formula for their safety is really very simple—"Go on as you began." Or, as we might put it, "Continue in the spirit of repentance and trust with which you first came to Christ." All kinds of false teachers are active in the world today and so we constantly need to keep Paul's commands (6–7) in mind.

## My Response

## Memory Point

Review Key Verse 2 (Gal. 4:4–7) along with Key Verse 9 (Col. 1:19–20).

## ☐ PRAY to apply God's Word

Pray for someone you know whose faith in Christ is wavering . . .

# 47

☐ **PRAY for insight into God's Word**
"O God, who hast thought us worthy of this blessing, that Thy Word daily sounds in our ears, let it not find strong hearts and iron minds, but so let us submit ourselves to Thee with the humility which becomes us, that we may truly feel Thee to be our Father. Amen" *(John Calvin)*.

☐ **READ Colossians 2:8–15**

☐ **MEDITATE on God's Word**

*Discovery*
**1.** What does the phrase "takes you captive" (8) reveal about false teachers? What was the nature of their attack (8)?

_____

_____

**2.** Who is the focus of Paul's counterattack on the false teachers (9–15)? State in one sentence Paul's answer to those false teachers troubling the Colossian church.

_____

_____

**3.** How does Paul describe Christ's accomplishment at the Cross? How do Paul's word pictures (14–15) give you insight into your fight against the power of evil?

_____

_____

_____

_____

**4.** What person or group that you know of today is attacking the Christian faith? Is your own faith being attacked in any way? If so, how? What must you do to counter it?

_____

_____

_____

_____

### Reflection

The word "fullness" (*pleroma*), which means "completeness," is very important in this letter. Think of it in three connections:

*"Fullness" as used by the enemies of Paul's teaching.* They said that the Christian message, as taught in the churches and by Paul, was incomplete and needed their teaching and ideas to give it fullness. So "fullness" became one of their slogans.

*"Fullness" as seen in Christ.* "All right," Paul said, "let's talk about 'fullness.' You want to know where it is? It's in Christ!" Paul had used the word "fullness" earlier in 1:19; now he used it again (2:9). All the fullness is in him!

*"Fullness" as experienced by the Christian.* "Completeness"—what a glorious truth. There it is, in verse 10: "And you have this fullness in Christ." Paul went on to spell it out (11–15): the old nature buried, the new nature raised up, alive in Christ, forgiven, triumphing with Christ over every foe. What more could we need? Having found Christ, we need look no further.

Paul was able to repel the confusing ideas of the false teachers, not so much because he was a more sophisticated theologian, but rather because he had a deep, personal relationship with the living Lord. And that's the best defense against error there is.

### My Response

### Memory Point

Review: Go over all your Key Verses from Philippians today.

### ☐ PRAY to apply God's Word

Ask the Holy Spirit to make your relationship with Jesus more real and alive in the next month . . .

# 48

□ **PRAY for insight into God's Word**
Quiet me, Father, as I approach your holy Word. Make me willing to accept the message you have waiting for me in these verses.

□ **READ Colossians 2:16–19**

□ **MEDITATE on God's Word**

*Discovery*
**1.** In these verses, Paul further describes the errors that were brewing in Colosse. What did these consist of (16–18)?

_____

_____

_____

**2.** What principle does Paul again lay down for evaluating such teaching (17, 19)?

_____

_____

**3.** Why is the metaphor of a body (19) helpful for seeing the effects of false teaching?

_____

_____

**4.** How do some people try to judge (16) and disqualify (18) the Christian commitment of others today? Is it ever appropriate to judge the faith of someone else? Are there situations where it would be wrong not to?

_____

_____

_____

_____

## Reflection

Any genuine Christian wants to grow in the knowledge of the Lord and in Christian life and service. Peddlers of new sects and heretical forms of Christianity often take advantage of this desire by implying that they have some new key to being one hundred percent Christian that everyone else has missed! This was another ploy the false teachers were using in Colosse. So the Colossian Christians encountered two conflicting messages about how to grow in their faith:

The *"sensational" way of the new teachers*. It was a mixture of Judaism (rules about food and drink, festivals, new moons, sabbaths), the occult (self-abasement, worship of angels, visions), and philosophy (gnostic asceticism). It all seemed new, exciting, and different, but it led nowhere then and its modern equivalents lead nowhere today.

The *"steady" way of Jesus Christ*. It seemed so ordinary, compared with the sparkle of the new ideas. But holding fast to the Head (Jesus) is in fact the only way to become a strong, overcoming, witnessing Christian. When the whole fellowship of Christians enters deeply into the mind of Christ, that is, the "growth that is from God" (19, RSV).

## My Response

## Memory Point

Repeat Key Verse 9 (Col. 1:19-20) when you are engaged in some routine activity today (washing dishes, dressing or undressing, etc.).

## ☐ PRAY to apply God's Word

Ask God to show you the area of your Christian life where he has been waiting for you to grow . . .

# 49

☐ **PRAY for insight into God's Word**
Begin your study by singing (or humming) the song which best expresses your feelings for God now.

☐ **READ Colossians 2:20–3:4**

☐ **MEDITATE on God's Word**

*Discovery*
**1.** What was Paul warning the Colossians about (20–22)? Why was their behavior so exasperating (20, 23)?

_____

_____

_____

**2.** What positive corrective does Paul offer to help the Colossians avoid these mistakes (3:1–2)?

_____

_____

**3.** One element of the false teaching was asceticism, which Paul describes as "false humility" (18, 23), "self-imposed worship" (23) and "harsh treatment of the body" (23). How is this seen among Christians today? Would you agree that the majority of Western Christians have gone to the opposite, and equally dangerous, extreme? If so, why?

_____

_____

_____

_____

**4.** What are some practical ways that you could "set your heart on things above" (3:2) in the coming week? What areas of your life or schedule would need to be adjusted if you were to obey this command?

_____

_____

_____

## Reflection

Knowing Christ as Lord elevates him above everything else in life. In contrast, legalism ministers to pride by setting up a program against which you check yourself. In Christian faith you relate not to a program but to Jesus Christ. In today's passage, this relationship is pinpointed by two emphases, spiritual headship (2:16–19), and spiritual liberty (2:20–23).

By spiritual headship, Christ releases us from ritualism, self-abasement or asceticism, from the worship of angels (and demons!), and from other legalistic requirements.

By spiritual liberty, we are dead to the old self-life by identification with Christ. A Christian ought to live neither by human rules nor by self-abasement, but by dedication to Christ and his work. The reward is a good self-image and a sense of true fulfillment.

While Jesus died to free us from our sins, he also rose again to introduce us to a new life—the resurrection life. In Colossians 3:1–4, we find a *new life* (1) because we are in fellowship with the risen Christ. There is *new longing (2)*, for our affection is centered on the things of Christ, not of the earth. God's cure for status seeking, power struggles, materialism, or sensuality is to have lives that center in Christ. There is *new love (3)*, for in contrast to the sinfulness of self-love, we share a new life "hidden with Christ in God." There is also *new living (4)*, for Christ is our life. He revealed God's will in what he said, what he did, and in what he was.

## My Response

## Memory Point

What insights have you gained from meditating on Key Verse 9 (Col. 1:19–20)?

## ☐ PRAY to apply God's Word

Pray about the one area where you most need to set your mind on "things that are above " . . .

# 10/Colossians 3:5–4:18
## Direction for Living

☐ **Introduction**

Whenever you make a major purchase, you receive an owner's manual to help you figure out how to use what you've bought. Such manuals usually begin with a review of the product's features and a reminder of how well your purchase will serve you. Then they begin to list the detailed instructions for usage.

For example, when you buy a car you get a fat owner's manual with information about where all the instruments and features are located, how to change a tire, how and when to perform routine maintenance, how to care for the car's appearance, where to go for replacement parts and many other practical items. A good owner's manual also includes a list of warnings: don't use leaded gasoline, don't run the car if a particular light in the dashboard comes on, don't carry more than a certain amount of weight. Car manufacturers realize that, although most car buyers basically know how to drive a car, special directions are necessary to insure that consumers properly use their cars and avoid problems.

The second half of Colossians is something like an owner's manual. Paul knew that the Colossians basically understood the Christian faith. But he also realized they needed a list of practical directions to help them put their faith into action and to avoid problems. And so he gave them one.

Paul's owner's manual begins with things not to do. He says, "Put to death, therefore, whatever belongs to your earthly nature"; that leads him into the specifics of two lists of "no-nos" for Christians (3:5–6, 8–9). Then he switches to the positive, things to "put on," as he says, and for several verses he lists what we *should* do as Christians.

In the middle of his owner's manual, Paul deals with an important special situation, Christian households. There are workable directions for husbands, wives, children, and even masters and slaves. Paul then completes his practical manual with some random general directions and a few personal greetings.

The problem with an owner's manual, however, is that it isn't always used correctly. If you reflect on three mistakes you can make in regard to an owner's manual, you will gain some insight on how to get the most out of the last portion of Colossians.

*Mistake #1–Failure to read the directions.* People who don't discipline themselves to read the Bible miss out on all the practical instructions God has spelled out there. You can't expect to live the Christian life successfully without it.

*Mistake #2–Failure to follow the directions.* Some people know what God's Word says but they just don't put it into practice. They don't act because they are too busy or lazy or forgetful. Whatever the excuse, however, it all boils down to disobedience.

*Mistake #3–Failure to trust the manufacturer.* Some people who know what the Bible says decide that they have a better way. "Oh, that part of the Bible is outdated," they say. But people who think like this (even if only subconsciously) are really saying, "I know better than God does," and are headed for deep spiritual trouble.

As you complete these next studies, you may think that the Scripture passages sound so familiar that you must have read them before. If so, you're right. About seventy percent of the material in Colossians is also found in the book of Ephesians. To help explain this fact, think again about an owner's manual for a car. Often one manual applies to several variations of the same car. One may be a convertible, one a station wagon, another a sedan, but they may all share the same kind of engine and drive-train and therefore can use the same owner's manual. When Paul wrote to the various churches, he addressed the special problems affecting each. But he could repeat a lot of his directions for Christian living because, whether his readers lived in Ephesus, Colosse, or even in the modern world today, the instructions never changed.

So don't skim through these final readings because you've studied the material before. Remember, Paul repeated these directions because they were especially important. Don't make a fourth mistake: attempting to follow the owner's manual without fully understanding it.

## ☐ Key Verse 10: Colossians 3:12–14
Therefore, as God's chosen people, holy and dearly loved, clothe yourselves with compassion, kindness, humility, gentleness and patience. Bear with each other and forgive whatever grievances you may have against one another. Forgive as the Lord forgave you. And over all these virtues put on love, which binds them all together in perfect unity.

## ☐ Outline

### Colossians: Focus on Christ

I. Correction for Error
   A. Thanksgiving and prayer  *1:1–14*
   B. Description of Christ  *1:15–23*
   C. Paul's situation  *1:24–2:7*
   D. Erasing errors  *2:8–3:4*

II. **Directions for Living**
   A. **Old and new habits  3:5–17**
   B. **Christian households  3:18–4:1**
   C. **Instructions and greetings  4:2–18**

# 50

☐ **PRAY for insight into God's Word**
Challenge me to a deeper obedience to you, Lord, through this passage of Scripture.

☐ **READ Colossians 3:5–11**

☐ **MEDITATE on God's Word**

*Discovery*
**1.** Into what general category do the sins listed in verse 5 fall? In your opinion, which one is the most difficult for you to resist? Why?

_____

_____

_____

**2.** Paul gives a second list of six sins (8–9). What is common to them all (see James 3:1–12)? How are you battling these temptations in your own life?

_____

_____

_____

**3.** If Paul knew you, and if he were writing this letter to you, what would he add to the list of things to "put off"? What should you do about these?

_____

_____

_____

**4.** What biblical principle does verse 11 express? Why is this an important principle? What other distinctions are eliminated in Christ (Gal. 3:28, James 2:1–7)?

_____

_____

_____

_____

## Reflection

Although the false teachers at Colosse were wrong to insist on all kinds of trivial rules and regulations (2:16-19), it is equally wrong to say that in the Christian life there are no rules or laws. Some things are always right and some are always wrong, and Paul gives two groups of examples.

*Unbridled desire (5-7).* No matter what form it takes, an uncontrolled giving in to our selfish desires should have no place in the Christian life. Paul gives examples (5) and tells us the result (6). Any person who professes to know Christ and who simply follows the demands of his or her own body is living a lie.

*Unloving discord (8-9).* Here are some other ways people put "self" first—all unfitting for Christians. The only way a Christian should relate to another person is by love, just as Christ himself did. Anything that contradicts love must be eliminated (8).

Every Christian has a "new nature" (10, RSV). We must do more than merely talk about it; we must act as if we really believed it.

Paul gives one way we can do this in the next verse. There can be no racial prejudice where Christ is honored (11). Are your attitudes and actions completely Christlike in this area? Is there a way you could work for racial harmony in your community?

## My Response

## Memory Point

Write Key Verse 10 (Col. 3:12-14) on a 3x5 card and place it in a familiar spot. Whenever you see it throughout the day repeat it several times.

## ☐ PRAY to apply God's Word

Pray about one way you could help the Holy Spirit overcome racial prejudice in your own life or in your neighborhood . . .

# 51

□ **PRAY for insight into God's Word**
"My soul yearns, even faints for the courts of the LORD; my heart and my flesh cry out for the living God" (Ps. 84:2).

□ **READ Colossians 3:12–17**

□ **MEDITATE on God's Word**

### Discovery
**1.** Why do you think Paul referred to the Colossians as "God's chosen ones, holy and dearly loved" (12)? Does the idea of being chosen by God motivate you to more or less action? Why?

_____

_____

_____

**2.** When do you experience the greatest amount of peace? What things erode your sense of peace?

_____

_____

**3.** If you can, write down the name of a person against whom you have a grudge. How could you obey verse 13 in regard to that person? Must you forgive someone who doesn't ask for forgiveness—or who doesn't even want it?

_____

_____

_____

**4.** List two new ways you can express Christian love (14) this week or this month.

_____

_____

_____

## Reflection

Here we are asked to do two different kinds of things—first, "Put on . . ." (12, 14); second: "Let . . ." (15–16). In the first case we take positive steps to do something; in the second we play a more passive part as we allow something to influence us. Both have their place in Christian discipleship.

*"Put on compassion, kindness, humility, gentleness, and patience" (12, TEV).* Here are five qualities that we Christians are to cultivate. Paul does not mean that we are to pretend we have them, putting them on like an actor's makeup. He means to cultivate them as a gardener cultivates flowers.

*"Put on . . . love" (14).* Love is like the string on which pearls are threaded; without it the Christian virtues tend to be an untidy mess; with it they are orderly and beautiful.

*"Let the peace of Christ rule" (15).* We cannot in any sense contribute to this; but we can open ourselves to Jesus Christ, in prayer and in trust, so that he controls our thoughts and words. His peace flows from absolute confidence in God, and is not affected by the changes and upsets of events.

*"Let the word of Christ dwell . . ."* Again, if we keep our minds and hearts open, remember his Word, and meditate on his commands, the results are bound to follow.

Verse 17 is positive and also challenging. Will you be involved in any activities or conversations this week that you'd be ashamed to do "in the name of the Lord Jesus"?

## My Response

## Memory Point

Face yourself in a mirror and practice Key Verse 10 (Col. 3:12–14) until you can say it three times in a row without a mistake.

## ☐ PRAY to apply God's Word

Ask God to use your reading of the Bible to alter your life and thinking this month . . .

# 52

☐ **PRAY for insight into God's Word**
Lord, make me willing and able to reorient my opinions according to your Word.

☐ **READ Colossians 3:18–4:1**

☐ **MEDITATE on God's Word**

*Discovery*
**1.** Which do you think is more difficult; for wives to be subject to their husbands or for husbands to love their wives (18–19)? Why?

_____

_____

_____

**2.** If you are a parent, how does verse 21 (compare Eph. 6:4) apply to you? What are some principles that could help keep a balance between demanding obedience and not "embittering" or "exasperating" your children?

_____

_____

_____

**3.** What tasks at work or home do you find most unpleasant? How do Paul's instructions in 3:22–4:1 apply? Do you think God considers you an enthusiastic worker (23)? Why or why not?

_____

_____

_____

**4.** In your opinion, what things are crucial for building a Christian family? What attitudes can destroy a Christian family? What is your responsibility to other families who are experiencing trouble?

_____

_____

_____

_____

### Reflection

Paul now addresses people in different kinds of relationships, and urges them to do everything "in the Lord." What a tremendous difference this will make!

*Not everyone has the same role to play.* There is resistance nowadays to any suggestion that people may have different roles and functions in home or society. But Paul shows that wives, husbands, children, parents, workers, employers, all have different duties and responsibilities. Are you comfortable with the role God has given you?

*But everyone has the same rules to obey.* Do you see how each group is told basically the same—to be gentle, considerate, honest and fair with those they are in contact with? You could sum it up in two words: love and respect. Love means understanding how the other person feels, trying always to support and never to hurt. Respect means remembering that the other person is your equal because he or she stands on a par with you before the Lord.

Often we take the attitude, "There's no way I can respect him until he changes his attitude towards me." But that position allows God's Spirit little room to work. If you are currently in a tense home or work situation, dare to start showing love and respect—regardless of what others do—and see how God begins to work.

### My Response

### Memory Point

Today write your own paraphrase of Key Verse 10 (Col. 3:12–14) on the back of the 3x5 card on which you first copied the verse.

### ☐ PRAY to apply God's Word

Pray for one parent/child relationship you know of that needs God's special attention now . . .

# 53

□ **PRAY for insight into God's Word**
Holy Spirit, transform these next few minutes into a living dialogue with my heavenly Father.

□ **READ Colossians 4:2-9**

□ **MEDITATE on God's Word**

*Discovery*
**1.** From verse 2, what two attitudes are to characterize our thoughts as we pray? Why should we be "watchful" (2)?

_____

_____

**2.** What tips about sharing your faith do you find in verses 5 and 6? What qualities of communication come to mind from the word picture "seasoned with salt"? Which of the ideas mentioned in verses 5-6 is the most challenging to you?

_____

_____

_____

_____

**3.** What "door" for ministry (3) would you like God to open for you? Why?

_____

_____

_____

**4.** List two or three ministers of the gospel whom you would like to especially pray for this month.

_____

_____

_____

## Reflection

In these short verses, Paul shows us how to deal with three important aspects of our Christian lives:

*Dealing with God (2–4).* There are four factors in prayer to consider here: two are concerned with our attitude in prayer ("steadfastly" RSV, "watchful"); and two with the content of our prayer ("thanksgiving," "pray for us, too"). "Watchful" suggests the sentry on the alert. Alert for what? Could it be for the voice of God answering our prayer? Do we make time to listen? "Pray for us," says Paul, reminding us not to be self-centered in our praying.

*Dealing with nonbelievers (5–6).* We must behave wisely, giving careful thought to our relationships with non-Christians; we have to remember that, though they may not read the Bible, they are "reading" us. "Seasoned with salt" suggests deliberately including in our talk "flavorful" comments that draw attention to God's place in the scheme of things.

*Dealing with one another (7–9).* Paul doesn't stop asking for their prayers—he takes care to supply them with information to help them pray (8). "Onesimus, our faithful and dear brother" (9), was in fact a slave who had run away from Colosse and come under Paul's influence in Rome. Paul said he was "one of them"; he had been "redeemed," implying that the Colossians should fully accept him. Here was an opportunity for the Colossian Christians to put into practice something that Paul had been preaching to them (3:11).

## My Response

## Memory Point

What new thing have you learned from Key Verse 10 (Col. 3:12–14)?

## ☐ PRAY to apply God's Word

Think about the nonbelievers you will see today. Ask the Holy Spirit to make you consciously aware of ways you could turn conversations toward spiritual things . . .

# 54

☐ **PRAY for insight into God's Word**
Father, let me sense the joy of seeking you and the satisfaction of finding you in these verses today.

☐ **READ Colossians 4:10–18**

☐ **MEDITATE on God's Word**

*Discovery*
**1.** What makes you assured in the will of God (12)? In what area are you currently in need of God's guidance so you can be more sure about his will for you?

_____

_____

_____

**2.** To see what happened to Demas' (14) ministry, see 2 Timothy 4:10. How can you safeguard against a similar consequence in your life?

_____

_____

_____

**3.** Are you in need of a reminder such as that in verse 17? Why? What is the work or area of responsibility you have received in the Lord?

_____

_____

_____

**4.** Why would Paul end this letter, "Remember my chains"? How do the sufferings of other Christians motivate you? How else should they?

_____

_____

_____

### Reflection

Here's a fascinating little glimpse of a varied group of first-century Christians. All different, yet each contributing to the life and growth of the body of Christ. Here are some of them:

*Aristarchus, sharing Paul's imprisonment.* Probably one of a group of Paul's friends who voluntarily took turns in sharing his prison cell.

*Mark, repenting and restored.* He had let Paul down on one of his journeys (Acts 15:37–38). But one failure is never the end; Mark made a new start.

*Epaphras, praying from far away.* Away from home, helping Paul, he could still play his part in the life of the Colossian church!

*Archippus, facing a task for God.* We don't know what it was; perhaps he had to give leadership while Epaphras was away. Now he must strengthen himself in God to fulfill the work God had entrusted to him.

*Paul himself, keeping faith even in prison.* So many were looking to him for leadership. His chains may have affected his handwriting (18), but not his spirit!

### My Response

### Memory Point

Review all the Key Verses listed on the last page of this book. Can you say them all straight through without error?

### ☐ PRAY to apply God's Word

Pray for Christians you know of who are suffering for the sake of Christ at this moment . . .

# *Prayer Notebook*

| date | request | date of answer |
|------|---------|----------------|
|      |         |                |

date    request                                                    date of answer

# God Is Speaking to Me About . . .

date

# Key Verses

*The verses printed below are from the New International Version.*

*Use the space below to copy the Key Verse from another version, if you wish.*

### Key Verse 1: Galatians 2:20
I have been crucified with Christ and I no longer live, but Christ lives in me. The life I live in the body, I live by faith in the Son of God, who loved me and gave himself for me.

### Key Verse 2: Galatians 4:4-6
But when the time had fully come, God sent his Son, born of a woman, born under law, to redeem those under law, that we might receive the full rights of sons. Because you are sons, God sent the Spirit of his Son into our hearts, the Spirit who calls out, "Abba, Father."

### Key Verse 3: Galatians 5:22-23
But the fruit of the Spirit is love, joy, peace, patience, kindness, goodness, faithfulness, gentleness and self-control. Against such things there is no law.

### Key Verse 4: Ephesians 2:8-10
For it is by grace you have been saved, through faith—and this not from yourselves, it is the gift of God—not by works, so that no one can boast. For we are God's workmanship, created in Christ Jesus to do good works, which God prepared in advance for us to do.

### Key Verse 5: Ephesians 4:15-16
Instead, speaking the truth in love, we will in all things grow up into him who is the Head, that is, Christ. From him the whole body, joined and held together by every supporting ligament, grows and builds itself up in love, as each part does its work.

***Key Verse 6: Ephesians 5:8-10***
For you were once darkness, but now you are light in the Lord. Live as children of light (for the fruit of the light consists in all goodness, righteousness and truth) and find out what pleases the Lord.

***Key Verse 7: Philippians 2:5-8***
Your attitude should be the same as that of Christ Jesus: Who, being in very nature God, did not consider equality with God something to be grasped, but made himself nothing, taking the very nature of a servant, being made in human likeness. And being found in appearance as a man, he humbled himself and became obedient to death—even death on a cross!

***Key Verse 8: Philippians 4:4-7***
Rejoice in the Lord always. I will say it again: Rejoice! Let your gentleness be evident to all. The Lord is near. Do not be anxious about anything, but in everything, by prayer and petition, with thanksgiving, present your requests to God. And the peace of God, which transcends all understanding, will guard your hearts and your minds in Christ Jesus.

***Key Verse 9: Colossians 1:19-20***
For God was pleased to have all his fullness dwell in him, and through him to reconcile to himself all things, whether things on earth or things in heaven, by making peace through his blood, shed on the cross.

***Key Verse 10: Colossians 3:12-14***
Therefore, as God's chosen people, holy and dearly loved, clothe yourselves with compassion, kindness, humility, gentleness and patience. Bear with each other and forgive whatever grievances you may have against one another. Forgive as the Lord forgave you. And over all these virtues put on love, which binds them all together in perfect unity.